Peace is Possible

Exchanging Weapons for Development

and how we disarmed the

Khmer Rouge

with wit, bluff --- and balloons

by Dr Robin Edward Poulton

WfD is a disarmament innovation that can transform post-conflict reconstruction:
the case of Cambodia

with a description of the specific Cambodian context
and analysis of Lessons Learned in many different countries
on collecting firearms and managing weapons.

Written and published in the hope that our experience will help all United Nations peace operations

In memory of Chou Bounine, a valued Cambodian friend and colleague

This story of peace building and disarmament is part of the EPES Mandala commitment to sharing information and analysing Lessons Learned from the field. For more Lessons Learned go to our website: http://www.epesmandala.com/publication_lessonsnew.php

EPES Mandala Consulting Ltd

presents **"PEACE IS POSSIBLE"** and the genesis of

Weapons for Development

**A disarmament innovation that transformed post-conflict reconstruction:
the case of Cambodia**

with a description of the specific Cambodian context
and Lessons Learned from many different countries
about collecting firearms and managing weapons

with a Preface by David de Beer

This study describes a project whose success was due to many different people: mainly Cambodians, with the help and leadership of a few Europeans working for the Council of Europe, and with support from United Nations agencies, and from the Dutch and Japanese governments as well as Canadian, French, German and British officials and from a bunch of non-governmental organisations without whose efforts the project would not have been successful. It is a tribute to the leadership of Henny van der Graaf and David de Beer.

This was the fruit of collective efforts by the people who created EPES Mandala Consulting as a company dedicated to promoting peace and to sharing Lessons Learned. It is in that spirit that we are publishing the story, in the hope that practitioners – particularly the European Union's diplomats, and the military, police and civilian professionals working in United Nations Peace Operations – will be able to find inspiration and ideas.

Written by Dr Robin Edward Poulton[1]
Managing Partner, EPES Mandala Consulting

---

[1] REP is a Senior Fellow of UNIDIR, the United Nations Institute for Disarmament Research in Geneva. He studied in St Andrews and Oxford in UK, before action-research with UNDP and UNICEF in Afghanistan – leading to his PhD in 1979 from EHESS in Paris (France). He has worked, written and taught extensively on African and Asian peace and development, consulting for EU, UN, bilateral government development agencies and many NGOs. He was sometime Visiting Professor at the European Peace University (Austria), at University of Richmond and at Virginia Commmonwealth University (USA), where he later became an affiliate faculty member in the VCU School of World Studies.

Acronyms

APSA	African Peace & Security Architecture established by the African Union
CMAC	Cambodia Mine Action Centre
CoC	Code of Conduct
CSBM	Confidence and Security Building Measures
CSO	Civil Society Organisation
DAC	Development Assistance Committee (OECD)
DDR	Disarmament, Demobilisation and Reintegration (see Note 2 below)
EOD	Explosive Ordnance Disposal
EC	European Commission
EU	European Union
EEAS	European External Action Service
EU-ASAC	EU Assistance on curbing Small Arms and light weapons in Cambodia
HKI	Helen Keller International (international NGO)
JICA	Japan International Cooperation Agency
JSAC	Japanese Assistance Team for Small Arms Management in Cambodia
KII	Key Informant Interviews
KR	Khmer Rouge
LFA	Logical Framework Analysis
MFA	Ministry of Foreign Affairs
MoD	Ministry of Defence
MoEF	Ministry of Economy and Finance
MoI	Ministry of Interior
MRRD	Ministry of Rural Reconstruction and Development
NCWMR	National Commission for Weapons Management and Reform (NatCom)
NGO	Non Governmental Organisation
NIP	EU's National Indicative Programme
OECD	Organisation for Economic Cooperation and Development (DAC)
OSCE	Organisation for Security and Cooperation in Europe
RCAF	Royal Cambodian Armed Forces
RDRDRDR	3D4R is a more complete version of DDR[2]
RGC	Royal Government of Cambodia
RMDS/G	Regional Micro-Disarmament Standards and Guidelines (SEE)
SAA	Small Arms Ammunition (Calibre 14.5mm and below)
SALW	Small Arms and Light Weapons
SAPS	SALW Perceptions Survey
SAS	Small Arms Survey (Geneva)
SEESAC	South Eastern and Eastern Europe Clearinghouse
SSR	Security Sector Reform
UN	United Nations
UNDDA	United Nations Department for Disarmament Affairs
UNDPKO	United Nations Department of Peacekeeping Operations
UNDP	United Nations Development Programme
UNPoA	UN Programme of Action on small arms and light weapons
VWCP	Voluntary Weapons Collection Programme
WCP	Weapons Collection Point
WED	Weapons in Exchange for Development
WfD	Weapons for Development (see Box 1 for other terms)
WGWR	Working Group for Weapons Reduction (Cambodian NGO)
VMG	Village Model Gardens
VMPF	Village Model Poultry Farms

---

[2] DDR is a misleading shorthand. The length and complexity of the process, and the need for the R to be planned before the D begins, is better rendered as 3D4R: Reintegration, Disarmament, Reconciliation, Demobilisation, Reinsertion, Destruction of weapons, Rehabilitation of the economy. Sometimes you also need context-specific R factors like Resettlement of Refugees; Retraining youth and the handicapped; and Recuperating girls who have been victims of sexual abuse. The vulnerable are too often neglected in traditional DDR military designs.

One of the Village Model Gardens launched by the EU-ASAC project to help the wives of local police to increase police family incomes in Kracheh Province, to make their husbands less dependent on bribes and extortion to feed their families. This innovation was a local NGO success-story with Helen Keller International. Some police wives even became horticultural extension agents, improving diets and incomes for communities involved in the weapons-for development campaign.

A great deal of helpful advice have been provided by Henny van der Graaf and David de Beer, both very successful Project Managers of EU-ASAC, to whom we owe the project's success, and who deserve warmest thanks. Photos from the author, from Henny and David, from Anna Fisher and from WikiCommons – all of whom we thank most sincerely.

Thanks also to my UNIDIR colleague Dr Valerie Yankey-Wayne whose professional brilliance has enhanced the text and its presentation; to then-UNIDIR Director Patricia Lewis who supported EU-ASAC; and to my lovely wife Dr Michelle Elcoat Poulton for eliminating many of my errors.

Great thanks also go to my friends and colleagues Juha Auvinen and Owen Greene, Seng Son, Kry Davuth, Dan Pisey and the EU-ASAC team without whose skills this project could never have taken place; to Rick Schroeder and Dr Sokha who made it happen in the villages; and to Adrian Wilkinson whose final evaluation was filled with insights.

Very best thanks also to my brilliant and creative editor Elisabeth Drumm, who made this new edition possible, and who found a new title for this second edition.

Peace is Possible

**Exchanging Weapons for Development and how we disarmed the
Khmer Rouge with wit, bluff --- and balloons**

CONTENTS

- **Preface**
- **Foreward to this Second Edition**
- **1- Introduction: WfD applies anthropology for peace**
- **2- The war history behind the peace story**
- **3- The story of WfD and SSR in Cambodia**
- **4- Lessons Learned from peace building in Cambodia**
- **5- Weapon management checklist**
- **6- Evaluating weapon programmes**

Box 1: The evolutionary jargon of weapon collection
Box 2: Telling the story of peace building
Box 3: Spending money efficiently
Box 4. Development and Disarmament – conflict or synergy?
Box 5. Mandala, symbol of harmony and sustainable peace

Preface

It is significant that Robin Poulton, the author of "Peace is Possible", calls this publication "a story". It is not called a history or a handbook, but just simply a story. And a story is always about people. Therefore this publication is also about people and it puts the question of disarmament and small arms control where it belongs – as part of a post-conflict peace process to bring security and development to the people who have suffered from the destructive violence of war and conflict. Small arms control is firstly about people and only after that is it about strategies, work plans and techniques.

Robin Poulton is eminently qualified to write such a story. He is one of the very few academics specialised in Small Arms who has extensive field experience developing, implementing and evaluating weapons control strategies. He has a unique ability to switch between the academic and field environments, thriving on the challenges of interacting with villagers and monks, but also unfazed by having to deal with corrupt officials who do not "play by the book". He has seen academic innovations tested in the field, but more importantly realises how pioneering strategies developed out of necessity under the pressure of work in the field can be analysed and fed back into concrete academic reflections.

The EU ASAC project in Cambodia was implemented between 1999 and 2006. However, the Lessons Learned from it are still relevant today. This publication ends with an invaluable list of Lessons Learned from Small Arms control projects and an innovative Check List for future Small Arms management projects. In doing so, this publication begins with a description of the communities in Cambodia holding illegal weapons, but who will finally hand them in for destruction and will benefit from the ensuing development. It is only after we have been introduced to the people who matter that Robin Poulton takes us on to the Lessons Learned and the techniques what can make weapons management and weapons collection a success.

Perhaps the final comment could be given after a quick visit to Phonm Penh, the capital of Cambodia: In 2012 it is a very different city from what it was when the EU ASAC project began. The bustling streets and markets, the skyscrapers and housing estates under construction and a relatively low crime rate indicate it is a city with a future. There are many people who will say that this would not have been possible without the financial and technical assistance given by EU ASAC to the Cambodian Government to get rid of the surplus arms. It is to be hoped that this story from Cambodia will assist others in similar situations to create their own peace and positively influence their own future development.

David de Beer

**Special Adviser to the European Union and
EU ASAC Project Manager 2002-2006**

Cambodia's economy is dominated by two great rivers: the Mekong and the Tonle Sap

Cambodians' most important source of protein is fish

Author's Foreword to "Peace is Possible"

A second edition of the EPES presentation on "Weapons for Development"

The EU ASAC project in Cambodia was implemented with remarkable success between 1999 and 2006. We decided to tell the story of this experience, which turned out to be the best civilian disarmament project ever (at that time). Other DDR processes before this had some good success, of course. The UN disarmament in Mozambique was successful in collecting and registering weapons, but it did not clearly distinguish the phases of disarmament, demobilisations and destruction (or decommissioning) of weapons. Once the weapons had been collected, diplomats from the five permanent members of the UN Security Council made the mistake of cutting funding and ending the project, leaving thousands of weapons in storage. Many of these weapons leaked into the criminal market, wreaking havoc on the unfortunate citizens of South Africa.[3]

The very first SALW disarmament experience – the first of many micro-disarmament projects studied and recorded by UNIDIR[4] - was undertaken by the Commonwealth Monitoring Force in Rhodesia/Zimbabwe (1979-1980), when freedom fighters were being brought out of the bush to establish their new country and – in many cases – to join the new Zimbabwe army. In this case the weapons were not destroyed: but a re-structured national army was able to take control of the collected weapons and keep them safe.

Taking firearms from freedom fighters is only one part of the micro-disarmament process: for – like in Cambodia – Zimbabwe's border lands (even today) remain some of the most heavily mined in the world. Government statistics reveal more than 1,550 people dead, more than 2,000 people injured and more than 120 000 cattle killed or injured from mine contamination since the struggle to liberate Rhodesia from white minority rule. Norwegian People's Aid reports that mine contamination continues to limit access to water, cross-border movement and land for agriculture: which is why we all fought to achieve the 1997 Ottawa Mine Ban Treaty.[5]

Lessons Learned from Zimbabwe, Mozambique and Cambodia are still relevant today. Research is vital and reading case studies is valuable: there are always lessons that can be applied elsewhere, even though every peace and disarmament context is different (and I have been involved in dozens of them).

The financial crisis of 2008, caused by corrupt western bankers who were never held to account, led to a world-wide recession. While we were able to publish our Weapons for Development study on the EPES Mandala website, we did not have the money during the recession to print and circulate copies to UN peace operations, and among EU embassies and defense ministries. We failed to persuade the European Union to publish this study.

---

[3] https://www.tandfonline.com/doi/abs/10.1080/03057079808708572?src=recsys ; Eric Berman: *Managing Arms in Peace Processes : Mozambique*. UNIDIR Disarmament and Conflict Resolution Project. United Nations Institute for Disarmament Research, Geneva: 1996. UNIDIR/96/26. ISBN 92-9045-113-0.
https://www.unidir.org/files/publications/pdfs/disarmament-and-conflict-resolution-project-managing-arms-in-peace-processes-mozambique-135.pdf

[4] Christopher Smith, Peter Batchelor, Jakkie Potgieter: *Small Arms Management and Peacekeeping in Southern Africa*. UNIDIR Disarmament and Conflict Resolution Project. United Nations Institute for Disarmament Research, Geneva: 1996. UNIDIR/96/21. ISBN 92-9045-112-2.
https://www.unidir.org/files/publications/pdfs/disarmament-and-conflict-resolution-project-small-arms-management-and-peacekeeping-in-southern-africa-137.pdf

[5] https://www.npaid.org/Our-Work/Countries-we-work-in/Africa/Zimbabwe/Humanitarian-Disarmament-in-Zimbabwe
The International Campaign to Ban Landmines (ICBL) was a multi-association civil society campaign that persuaded governments to sign the Ottawa Treaty in October 1997, a legal convention to ban anti-personel landmines signed by more than 120 countries. The ICBL and its coordinator Ms Jody Williams were awarded the 1997 Nobel Peace Prize. https://www.nobelprize.org/prizes/peace/1997/icbl/history/

Learning Lessons is not something the EU is good at. Holding meetings: yes. Writing complex position papers: yes. Learning lessons from the field: not so much. EU staff are very intelligent, highly educated and many believe this gives them superior knowledge. The problem seems to be even greater among EEAS diplomats working in EU embassies across Africa: because their academic diplomas provide them with "knowledge" …. they do not seek "truth". Diplomats are often destabilized when they are confronted by practical problems and cultural differences that challenge their preconceptions, elements over which they have no control.

I am reminded of a very charming German Ambassador in West Africa during the extreme Sahelian drought of the 1970s, who was irritated when I explained to him that nomads receiving European Union food aid had no idea how to cook the strange cereals they had received. "Wenn man Hunger hat, dann wählt man nicht die Speisekarte," responded the Ambassador: showing appalling contempt for starving people, comparing them to plump Europeans studying the comfortable menu in a German restaurant. People were dying of starvation, and His Excellency was quite unable to understand their problems. These starving people were not "refusing" food, but confused by what to do with (how to prepare and eat) the inappropriate food that he was sending them. Worse, he did not want to know. He did not care.

By re-issuing our Weapons for Development story thanks to the new publishing opportunities offered by Amazon, we can show the world that "Peace is Possible." We hope that the lessons of our experience will reach a wider audience of Asian, African, American and European officials and peace workers. We hope that the dedicated staff in United Nations peace operations will use this story as a manual for new ideas, and distribute widely to its field practitioners - and especially to the military cohorts that arrive with little peace-preparation from countries all across the world - these Lessons Learned from the field.

If practitioners read our story about an unusual EU development and disarmament success in Cambodia, they may be able to work out new ways to transfer these lessons to their own conflict zone. "Peace is Possible" almost everywhere: but can you work out creative ways to achieve peace and disarmament in the special political and cultural circumstances in which you are working? That is the challenge of governments and peace workers everywhere.

It is all in the service of peace, development and economic justice.

Robin Edward Poulton (April 2020)

Peace is Possible

Exchanging Weapons for Development and how we disarmed the Khmer Rouge with wit, bluff --- and balloons

1- Introduction

The innovation of exchanging Weapons for Development.
Applying anthropology to disarmament and peace building.

Weapons for Development (WfD) was first tested by the UNDP in Albania in a project led by General Henny van der Graaf (retired from the Royal Dutch Army), then tried by Henny in Mali and later with remarkable success in Cambodia under the EU-ASAC project (1999-2006).[6] In Cambodia, we literally exchanged weapons for development projects chosen by the villagers, creating a model and learning lessons that others can apply. For WfD you need a favorable political context, a professional mechanism to collect weapons, and also a professional mechanism to deliver development – practices that demand teams with totally different skills, but who need to work together. When a colonel tries to deliver development, the result is pretty unconvincing as we discovered in Cambodia[7]; and non-professionals equally should keep out of the weapons business.

WfD has become a familiar 21st century strategy, undergoing exciting adaptations in different cultures. In former Yugoslavia, in an urban setting, WfD became 'cars for weapons' through a national lottery organised by SEESAC[8]: weapons were surrendered in exchange for lottery tickets to win a luxury motor car, supported by an intensive advertising campaign that would be difficult to imagine in a rural environment. We have been involved in numerous WfD projects in West Africa, and with UNIDIR we were active in mobilizing civil society in support of the 1998 ECOWAS Moratorium of Small Arms, which was a seminal event in peace building and helped create conditions for ending civil wars in Liberia and Sierra Leone. Weapons need to be licensed and controlled, and kept out of criminal hands. WfD is one mechanism for achieving this objective after a civil war. In the 1990s WfD was a new concept. This story describes how we invented, more or less from scratch in post-civil war Cambodia, a WfD project to collect up Khmer Rouge weapons along the Ho Chi Minh Trail.

The EU-ASAC programme developed a multi-facetted, integrated approach of which WfD was only one piece. That is important. The programme assisted the Royal Government of Cambodia (RGC) to strengthen the legal framework, improve weapons management in the security forces, collect weapons from villagers and implement extensive public awareness campaigns throughout the country. Components involving Security Sector Reform and Commune Council training in weapons security were also developed, while local police were trained and equipped and civil society strengthened. Our story also shows how, once officials became sensitised to the benefits of post-conflict weapon security, the RGC came to realise that Cambodia could play a leading part in improving regional and international security, and in the UN Programme of Action against illegal small arms.

---

[6] EU-ASAC (European Union Assistance on Curbing Small Arms and light weapons in Cambodia) was set up under European Union Council Decision 1999/730/CFSP of 15 November 1999 and started operations in April 2000. For more than six years EU ASAC assisted the Royal Cambodian Government and the project can be studied on the active website www.eu-asac.org.

[7] The colonel contracted local NGOs to build wells, but without defining 'a well' in terms of materials, depth, width or the amount of water the well should contain in the dry season. This produced several dry holes. Iraq and Afghanistan have shown the United States military floundering as they try to 'deliver development'. US Colonels in Afghanistan were building schools at five times the cost of an NGO school; the excess profits fed corruption and strengthened the financial power of local warlords who owned the construction companies.

[8] SEESAC: South East Europe Small Arms Campaign see www.seesac.org

Box 1: The evolutionary jargon of weapon collection

Every business develops its jargon, including the business of micro-disarmament (a term developed by the United Nations to cover the special problems of removing small arms and light weapons = SALW). Voluntary Weapons Collection Programmes (VWCP) have evolved new methods in different settings and cultures. The following names have been used so far, and more varieties will surely emerge:

'Weapons for Development' WfD – the term used originally in Albania and Cambodia
'Weapons in Exchange for Development' (WED)
'Weapons for Wells' (WfW) used in Cambodia as a cheaper version of WfD
'Weapons for roads for food' used in Cambodia by EU-ASAC and WfP to leverage WfD
'Weapons in Competition for Development' (WCD) where communities compete for projects
'Weapons Linked to Development' (WLD) which links existing projects with weapon collection
'Weapons in Exchange for Incentives (WEI) such as lottery tickets
'Guns for tools' : in exchange for a weapon, ex-fighters can receive production tools (like a plow)
'Guns for food' – offered to families or communities. This runs the risk of giving a 'value' to weapons, but is a better idea than 'buy-back' because giving cash actually increases the market for used weapons. We recommend from multiple experiences, that cash should never be offered for weapons.

2- The war history behind the peace story

Cambodia had been at war for thirty years, when the United Nations was given the task in 1993 of rebuilding the country. The Paris peace agreement was signed by all competing political and military parties, creating conditions for peace under the constitutional rule of King Norodom Sihanouk, the remarkable leader who had negotiated independence from the French in 1953.

When the French pulled out of their colony of Vietnam, the Americans moved in - ignoring the advice of General de Gaulle to stay away from Vietnam. As the US Air Force bombed the villages and forests of Vietnam, the independence fighters of North Vietnam – nationalist and communist Vietcong under their leader Ho Chi Minh - began moving their supplies on foot and by bicycle along the Cambodian forest trails of Kracheh Province and into South Vietnam. Cambodian ports also supplied the aggressive Vietnamese military machine, as Sihanouk's Cambodia balanced precarious neutrality between nationalist Vietcong and imperialist Americans. In March 1969, US Secretary of State Henry Kissinger started bombing neutral Cambodia[9], and launching helicopter raids inside the country. On 18 March 1970, the CIA made the mistake of encouraging their agent General Lon Nol to overthrow the God-like ruler Sihanouk. Overnight, the tiny Cambodian Communist Party – the Khmer Rouge - became a symbol of resistance to Lon Nol. Sihanouk has been given a bad press in the West because he resisted both French and American imperial ambitions; but he emerges from history as a Great Leader – especially when compared to the corrupt puppet general Lon Nol.[10]

---

[9] It was this brutal bombing of a neutral country that led to Henry Kissinger being denounced as a war criminal.

[10] The literature on Cambodia is vast. The following three books will provide a good understanding of the history: Elizabeth Becker: *When the war was over – Cambodia's revolution and the voices of its people,*. Simon & Schuster, New York: 1986; David Chandler: *Brother No 1, a biography of Pol Pot.* Silkworm Books, Bangkok: 1993; May Someth: *Cambodian Witness – the Autobiography of Someth May.* Random House, New York: 1986.

On 17 April 1975, the Khmer Rouge entered Phnom Penh - from which Lon Nol fled by helicopter. A disastrous Khmer Rouge experiment in socio-economic engineering then killed maybe one million Khmer - which some people describe as 'genocide'. Having driven the Americans out of Saigon in 1975, the North Vietnamese invaded Cambodia in December 1978 to end the Khmer Rouge terror. The West could not forgive the defeat of US troops in Vietnam. Despite the horrors of Khmer Rouge rule, Pol Pot and his genocidal cronies received financial and military support from the US, British and Chinese governments until the 1990s. Even after the UN-led transition of 1993, the Khmer Rouge held out and civil war rumbled on through the Cambodian forests. Fighting finally stopped in 1999. Shortly after the shooting stopped (as a matter of fact, thre was still residual shooting when EU-ASAC started work in the field), the EU Council approved a Cambodian disarmament programme[11] and recruited General Henny van der Graaf to help stabilise the country.[12]

Cambodia's Prime Minister, Hun Sen, had signed Decree No. 38 in 1998, declaring civilian weapons illegal. In the cities, the police collected weapons in roadblocks and house-to-house searches; but there were said to be more than one million weapons out there in rural Cambodia, and peace would stabilize only if people stopped shooting each other.

The EU-ASAC strategy document provided for assistance with drafting and implementing a weapons law, but General Henny decided it was urgent also to improve the management of government armouries[13] and collect illegal civilian weapons in rural areas, offering development projects to villagers in exchange for their weapons. His WfD success in one Albanian district had been mixed; but as the new EU Special Advisor for Disarmament in Cambodia, he thought a weapons-for-development collection scheme could work in Cambodia. Two pilot WfD programmes were launched, in Kracheh and Pursat provinces, funded by the Dutch and Japanese governments.

---

[11] Our EU project's formal title was *Assistance on curbing Small Arms and light weapons in the kingdom of Cambodia* = EU ASAC was authorised as EU Council Joint Action 1999/730/CFSP.
[12] The original project was designed by Dr Owen Greene, a peace specialist at Bradford University.
[13] The EU-ASAC project evolved into a comprehensive Security Sector Reform project, which was the main reason for its success. All government armouries tend to 'leak' – especially if there are no records of weapon and ammunition stocks. We worked with army, gendarmerie, police and finally even established weapon management systems for the naval and air forces. See the website www.eu-asac.org

This is a photo of collected weapons stored in a police lock-up in Sisophon. In the absence of any records, neither the numbers nor the types of weapons were known, even to local commanders. The poor security is emphasised by the flimsy nature of the building, which has daylight creeping in through gaps between the wooden boards. This is one of many weapon stores in Cambodia that illustrated the urgent need to record and destroy surplus weapons.

Wherever you go in Cambodia (here in Seam Reap) there will be people who lost a limb during the thirty years of civil war …. Or who were victims - after the war - to a landmine or a bomb left over from fighting.

Around the jungles of Cambodia you frequently find medieval temples overgrown by trees; and many of these temples were booby-trapped with mines and grenades by the Khmer Rouge. So watch your step!

3- The story of WfD and SSR in Cambodia

The objectives of our innovative disarmament project

Every project has declared objectives, and a broader, undeclared political vision (sometimes there are several visions, because different stakeholders have different hopes and fears). American, Russian and Chinese weapons had flooded into Cambodia during thirty years of war, and international political leaders saw this vast reservoir of weapons as a threat to more than just Cambodia: revolutionary and criminal armed movements all over Asia would be supplied from Cambodia unless the government could get control of the country and impose security.[14] One part of this challenge was to help the new civilian government gain control over the Cambodian military after thirty years of war.

The broader questions are universal. After the military and political battles have ceased, how does a government stop people using their weapons for criminal activity? How can any government (in post-conflict Cambodia, Northern Ireland, Mexico, Congo, Libya or Afghanistan) control a country where warlords are running protection rackets, where young men raised with weapons in a land of violence refuse to respect the elected or traditional leaders in their communities?

In the Cambodian context, young men had known no other form of lifestyle than warfare. The rural areas of post-conflict Cambodia were run by warlords with the title of Colonel or General, who had adopted the uniform of a new national army without any of its discipline. Some of them were former Khmer Rouge guerrillas. In every Province, civilian Governors had been appointed by the Minister of the Interior (who was also Deputy Prime Minister) but the most powerful person *de facto* was the Provincial Military Commander with his own troops, his own weapons and who did not report to the Governor, nor even to the Ministry of Defence, but to a poorly-structured and independent Military High Command in the distant capital city of Phnom Penh.

That was the situation in 1999. Peace was precarious. Roaming gangs of ex-fighters terrorised the countryside, kidnapping villagers for ransom. Kalashnikovs were still firing in every province and every district. The Khmer Rouge heavy guns had barely stopped firing when we arrived in Phnom Penh. WfD was the mechanism that started a peace dialogue in Eastern Cambodia, setting in motion a process that would remove terror from the minds of every villager.

General Henny assigned to me the task of collecting civilian weapons. I read every book I could find on Cambodian culture and on the period of Khmer Rouge violence, trying to understand this post-conflict country. I visited the torture chambers of Tuol Sleng and the killing fields at Choeung Ek. I studied Cambodian history and the caste system of medieval Angkor Wat. Soon after arriving in Phnom Penh from West Africa, I was my desk in the Golden Gate Hotel, beginning to design a WfD peace argument:

1) What is peace? Well, peace cannot involve firearms, because weapons make war!
2) Peace is a cultural phenomenon; there is no universal definition of peace. In a culture of violence, 'peace' may include plenty of stuff that other cultures might not accept.

---

[14] Indeed we heard in several Cambodian villages that Vietnamese arms dealers had already come around buying weapons, to be reconditioned for clandestine sales to the Philippines and Sri Lanka.

In Texas, Arizona and in Afghanistan, people see rifles as part of peace. Not in Cambodia: the new PM of Cambodia has signed Decree No 38 making firearms illegal.

3) Peace is having adequate food, good health and happy children.
4) If your family is hungry or sick, you do not have peace – that argument, I thought, should ring true in this society where poverty is rife, and physical security uncertain.
5) So can we establish that PEACE is all about food and health and happiness … ?
6) If so, then weapons and explosives must contribute to disturbing that peace.
7) So weapons and explosives are bad: if we want peace, we must give up all firearms.
8) Other people's illegal firearms and explosives are dangerous, and so are your own.
9) If you hand over illegal weapons to the police, they will be destroyed and you will see peace growing stronger because Cambodia will have fewer weapons than today.
10) If you give up your weapons, we will offer you something in exchange that contributes to peace as we have defined it together: for example, a development project to improve food or health. That is, we will exchange your Weapons for Development.

Kracheh Province, Cambodia, 1999

Kracheh is a French colonial town. A road runs along the bank of the mighty Mekong River, flanked by elegant buildings that look out over crowds of motorbike taxis. The motorboat from Phnom Penh brought us to the foot of a high staircase, reached across two precarious wooden planks. We waded through the throng of people and packages, dodged a few motorbikes and crossed the road to check in at the Hotel Santepheap - the Peace Hotel. Henny van der Graaf and Dennis Brennan (our lawyer) led the mission, met the Governor, and returned to Phnom Penh…. Abandoning me to an evening of Khmer karaoke with Major Davuth.

The second day, after formal meetings with the Governor, Davuth and I set off for our first WfD visit to rural communities along the Eastern Frontier. Through those trees, a few miles and a thousand landmines away, lay Vietnam. The delegation was led by His Excellency Soem Son, the First Deputy Governor of Kracheh Province. With him travelled the Provincial Commanders of the Army, the Gendarmerie and the Police – three extremely senior colonels, political rivals, quite possibly former enemies in this land of multiple armies and alliances. These were powerful men commanding barracks filled with men and guns. None of them had ever visited these remote rural villages. With them was Colonel Mao, head of a bodyguard of twenty armed soldiers to protect the Governor and his guest *Lok Europ*.[15] The whole mission was based around me. In these rural zones along the Ho Chi Minh Trail, wearing my EU-ASAC T-shirt and a badge showing the shining stars of Europe on a blue background, I had become *Lok Europ*, the *de facto* representative of the European Union.

Dusk was falling as our official provincial delegation arrived in *Wat* Pir Thnou.[16] Leaving my shoes on the pagoda steps, I crawled over the wooden floor behind the Deputy Governor towards the altar and touched my head five times on the mats. Candles, streamers and coloured balloons surrounded a giant, bronze-coloured Buddha, and small statues showing the nine positions (or were they manifestations?)

---

[15] *Lok* is a Khmer courtesy title, equivalent to 'Honourable Mister'.
[16] *Wat* means 'pagoda, and this building provides the central meeting point for rural Khmer society.

of the Lord Buddha. Having honoured the Lord Buddha, the Governor swivelled on his knees and bowed three times to a young monk wearing a big smile. I watched carefully, bowed three times to the young monk, and settled uncomfortably onto one buttock. I wanted to sit cross-legged. I knew I could sit for hours on end cross-legged with my elbows resting on my knees, but in Cambodia only monks were allowed to sit in the position of the Lord Buddha. Out of respect, the rest of us sat twisted.

Deputy Governor Soem Son explained the purpose of our visit and thanked the monk and the elders *achar* for their hospitality. Unable to follow his elaborate Khmer, with its special vocabulary for monks, I had time to study the young monk. I knew the monk had not eaten since 11am, and he would not eat again until tomorrow. This probably explained why Meah Nou (like most Khmer monks) was a chain smoker, and constantly sipped sweetened tea. In Vietnam Buddhist monks never smoke, but they ride motorbikes. Cambodian monks never ride motorbikes - they always sit side-saddle on the pillion behind the driver - but they are all heavy smokers.

Next morning, after an excellent breakfast of noodle soup, the Deputy Governor and I leaned on the balustrade of the pagoda with Chou Bounine, our new WfD Provincial Field Manager and translator, and watched villagers arriving for our very first meeting. Some came on foot, others on bicycles, in bullock carts, or crushed together on a motorbike carrying four passengers. One group arrived on a tractor. There were old and young, women with children, old men leaning on sticks …. and groups of young men wearing black pyjamas and the red *krama* bandanna of the Khmer Rouge. These were going to be the toughest people to convince: the men with guns who had known no life other than war.

Excellency Soem Son spoke to the assembled villagers of Pir Thnou area. He now used a simpler form of language, dropping the elaborate Khmer vocabulary reserved for monks, and I could at least recognize some Khmer words. Each of the colonels stood up as the Governor introduced him, and all too soon it was my turn. *Lok Europ* had centre stage, and 350 faces looked expectantly at the white man with the white beard.

My first disarmament speech in Cambodia began with the usual Khmer greetings. I kneeled up so that my head and shoulders were visible to all the villagers seated on the wooden planks of the Pir Thnou pagoda floor, pressed my hands together, and greeted the three hundred and fifty assembled villagers with, *"Chum reap sur. Sob sobay teh?"*

They returned the greetings, confirmed they were in good health, and looked expectant. I pointed to *Lok* Chou Bounine, and told them he was a wise man, a teacher, and smart enough to speak Khmer – unlike me! That got a laugh. Bounine stood up and told them my name: *Lok Europ,* the personal representative of the entire European Union. Not one of them had ever heard of the European Union, but it didn't matter. I was a guest and honoured to be visiting beautiful Wat Pir Thnou. They were pleased.

Mr Chou was a respected Kracheh teacher: formerly a teacher of French, proud of his mastery of "la langue de Voltaire." Now in his sixties, he had survived the Khmer Rouge years by pretending to be an illiterate cowherd, while his brother (a doctor) had been tortured to death. I admired Chou Bounine immensely.[17] With *Lok* Chou Bounine translating, I apologized for my ugly white face and my long nose with the hideously big nostrils. The villagers roared with laughter. Bounine and I were saying exactly what they were thinking! Some of these villagers had never seen a white man; few of them had ever been close to a *barang;* every one of them thought I was ugly. But of course, I announced with a gleam in my eye, I would never have to apologise to the people of *Wat* Pir Thnou for my beautiful, thick white beard. Three hundred and fifty villagers rolled around on the pagoda floor shaking with laughter. Even the monks and the young men in black pyjamas were laughing now. How would the villagers like to have a beard like mine, asked Bounine, pointing to me kneeling up on the floor, pulling my beard to emphasise the thickness of the growth. No Khmer could hope to have such a chin as mine. The straggly hairs growing from the chins of the *achar =* elders offered a feeble contrast with my thick white beard.

While Bounine worked the crowd, I checked the governor and the colonels. They were laughing as much as the villagers. Behind them sat Rick Schroeder and Dr Sokha[18] with some of their NGO development workers: without their expertise, we could not deliver the development projects. They – and the police - were our essential partners in this disarmament enterprise, and they all seemed to be having a good time. Like the half-dozen members of the local police force, the local army garrison of a dozen men and their lieutenant were also smiling. I sensed that the warm-up session was going well.

It was time to move to more serious matters. I pointed to sheets of paper that Bounine had pinned to the wooden pillars of the pagoda earlier that morning. 'What is peace?' asked the first poster, in Khmer writing. The drawings illustrated a world familiar to the villagers of Pir Thnou: a bullock cart, trees and vegetables and sacks of rice, bowls of noodles, children and clinics and houses on stilts. Major Davuth was a good artist.

"This is your life," I cried, "it looks happy and peaceful. Look at the trees in this picture heavy with fruit, the sacks filled with the rice harvest, the animals contented and well fed. But if your children are hungry when they go to sleep, are you at peace?"

"NO!" groaned 350 voices of people who knew all about hunger.

"And if your wife or your mother or your children are sick, can your family be at peace?"

"*Ateh!*" the villagers chorused. "There is no peace in a house with sickness."

"So what is peace? Peace is having food to eat, families who are not hungry, medicines when your mother is sick, and education for your children in schools which are clean and free of land mines."

---

[17] *Lok* Chou Bounine, a fine man, died on 19th June 2009 and this essay is dedicated to his memory.

[18] Leaders of a Non-Governmental Organisation called Partners for Development (PfD), which had continued working in Kracheh Province throughout the war years. PfD had organised the villagers and had created village development plans in partnership with every community in the area. It was this preparation that enabled us to implement our WfD efficiently throughout Kracheh, in partnership with PfD and local government services.

Bounine's translation reinforced the message. He sounded convincing to me, although I could not understand what he said; but he certainly held the attention of the audience with his eloquence. They obviously liked him, and listened with respect to his every word.

While Bounine was speaking, a baby started crying. Other small children were restless; one two-year-old was crawling over its mother and getting on her nerves. I rose from my knees, and picked my way through the crowd on my stockinged feet until I reached the restless child. 350 people watched with bated breath: was the *barang* a child-abuser? From the side pocket of my long pants, I produced a handful of colored balloons. I chose a red one for the two-year old, and handed it over gravely with two hands, showing maximum respect. Attracted by the red balloon even more than he was terrified by my white beard, the small boy reached up and took the balloon. His mother immediately made him thank me with a respectful two-handed *sompheat* gesture of respect. The crowd found it delightful. Quickly I padded round all the small children, handing out balloons, and the Pir Thnou peasants clapped and laughed as two dozen small children were cajoled into taking balloons and bowing respectfully with the *sompheat* gesture to *Lok Europ.* There were no more restless children, and we had established a new level of friendship.

"If poverty is the source of insecurity, how can a weapon make you more secure?" By now, everyone was agreed that food and health and education were the ingredients of 'peace and security'. So what was the role of weapons? "If security is a matter of good food and good health, then what is the role of firearms? Weapons cannot bring you security – they bring you insecurity!"

To support our argument, Bounine and I told stories of small children finding dangerous weapons, of babies blowing themselves up with their father's hidden hand grenade. My EU-ASAC colleague, Major Kry Davuth, was a fine artist and his drawings of exploding landmines and hand grenades were vivid; but no one in this pagoda needed reminding about the danger of explosives. Cambodia had the highest concentration of mines anywhere in the world, worse even than Angola and Afghanistan. During our meeting I heard a distant explosion and I prayed that it was a pig, and not a child, who had stepped on that landmine.

But now I had to persuade the villagers to surrender their weapons. The young men in black pyjamas at the back of the crowd had known nothing other than war since their birth. An AK47 assault rifle was their friend and their prestige. How was I going to persuade them to listen?

"So if you find a weapon hidden in the forest, what should you do? Should you leave it there because it is not yours? No, you should bring it to the Commune Chief so he can give it to the police to be destroyed. If you leave it in the forest, it could be found by a child and cause an accident. It could be used by a kidnapper, to kill your wife or your mother. Always remember this: an illegal firearm does not know the name of its owner; it knows only the name of its victim." This was a proverb I had composed in Phnom Penh. We had practised the Khmer version, which rolled smoothly off Bounine's tongue, *"a vuth man skorl chhmuos roborse via te, via skorl chhmuos te meak rong kruos punos,"* and he repeated the proverb several times during every meeting. Repetition makes a proverb stronger.[19] The villagers would carry that proverb home to their families.

"I am asking you to bring in the weapons so that they can be destroyed by the competent military authorities. What am I offering to you in exchange for the weapons? I am offering peace – and peace has no price. Peace is good food, good health, education and tranquility. To help you achieve peace, I will offer you development projects for your community: you will hand over your weapons, and in exchange the European Union will give you a well or a school or whatever project your community needs to achieve peace and progress."

We had no budget for any of these things, I remembered: raising the development funds was my next task when I returned to Phnom Penh …. But I could not allow a lack of resources to block my arguments for peace.

"And how many weapons must you bring us for a well or a school? There is only one answer: you must bring us ALL your weapons, for only when there are no illegal firearms and explosives, no more rockets and grenades and bullets in your houses, only THEN will you feel safe and only then will you find peace. I do not know how many weapons are hidden in your community, in the forest, in the rice paddies, in the thatched roofs of your houses and under the straw mattresses where you sleep: only YOU know how many weapons there are, and therefore only you can tell me how many weapons should be collected and destroyed, in order to bring peace to your communities."

I sensed it was time for me to hand the meeting over to the Governor and his colonels. I had made my argument, and now their words must reinforce mine. This was the most delicate part of the whole presentation. I had to stage-manage the colonels, hold them responsible, make them promise better security in front of the population of Pir Thnou, and in front of the Governor.

"If you give up your weapons, of course you need protection against robbers and bandits," I cried from my increasingly painful kneeling position. "You must receive this protection from the police. Excellency Soem Son has brought the Chief of Police of Kracheh Province here to speak with you, to promise you better protection from his police officers." I looked at the Police Colonel, who smiled wryly back at me.

"We all know that sometimes soldiers misuse their weapons, and Excellency Soem Son has brought the Army Commander of Kracheh Province here to speak with you, to tell you about the discipline of soldiers and the rules governing the use of weapons." I looked across at the Army Colonel, who glared back at me. "When they have spoken, you will ask them questions, and they will respond. If you have worries, the government officials will give you answers. Then, when you have heard the Colonels and when you have heard Excellency Soem Son, you will understand that tomorrow we will all be living in a New Cambodia where no one needs firearms. And always, always remember this truth: an illegal firearm does not know the name of its owner; it

---

[19] While the proverb was aimed at the general population, emphasising the danger of firearms and grenades for the lives of children and families, the message resonated with the security forces: any weapon falling into criminal hands might put their lives at risk. Five years later the EU-ASAC Final Evaluation (p18) concluded from a series of Key Informant Interviews, that weapon collection and denunciation in the villages was motivated by fear of being caught with an illegal firearm, closely followed by their awareness of the dangers of hidden weapons and of the negative influence of firearms on the economy (farmers were fearful of being kidnapped, while working in their fields, and so vital food crops were not being weeded or harvested).

knows only the name of its victim." Once again the proverb rolled smoothly off Bounine's tongue, *"a vuth man skorl chhmuos roborse via te, via skorl chhmuos te meak rong kruos punos."*

I turned to the Governor, and bowed. Excellency Soem Son grinned happily, and congratulated *Lok Europ* on his humour as well as the lucidity of the presentation. I grinned back, as Bounine whispered the translation into my ear. I had counted on laughter to bring me into contact with Cambodians, and I had been right. My reputation as an entertainer became known throughout Kracheh Province.

The Governor designated the Chief of Police to make his speech. Colonel Seng was a cheerful fellow, and he spoke rather well (or at least so it seemed to me, sitting at last on one buttock and nursing my bruised kneecaps; I should have brought a cushion). The Police Colonel spoke about the importance of the law. He told his audience about Decree No 38 signed in 1998 by Prime Minister Hun Sen, outlawing unregistered weapons in Cambodia. This was probably the first time anyone in Pir Thnou had heard about Decree No 38, including the local police contingent. It was therefore the first time it would have occurred to many people, that their AK47 left over from their years in the army might now get them into trouble.

The most important speech was yet to come: from the Army Colonel. Everyone in Cambodia knew that most crimes were committed by people in army uniform, by people who had temporarily removed their army uniform, or by friends of people in the army who were illegally borrowing an army rifle and using army ammunition to go hunting, steal water buffalo, kidnap people for ransom, or establish illegal roadblocks where they extorted 'taxes' from motor vehicles. Within the past month in this very same Snuol District where we were holding our meeting, within a few miles of Pir Thnou there had been an incident where three illegal roadblocks had been established on the same afternoon, one each by police, gendarme and army personnel. Not surprisingly, the ransomed truck drivers objected and the day ended in a firefight between the army and the gendarmerie.

The police colonel sat down. The army colonel rose to his feet with great reluctance. The Governor was using me, and I was happy to be his instrument. Under the neutral flag of the European Union, the provincial army chief was about to make an official and very public statement in front of Excellency Soem Son, First Deputy Governor of the Province of Kracheh – and if he messed up, the colonel might lose his job.

"Excellency First Deputy Governor Soem Son," began the speech …. The colonel was clear and formal. Decree No 38 had been signed by the Prime Minister, and soldiers were bound to obey it. This was the new law of the land. When soldiers returned home at night from the barracks, they should leave their rifles and ammunition in the barracks. Any soldier who was found carrying a firearm 'after hours' should be arrested by the police, and would serve 6 months in prison.

The speech was greeted in stunned silence. Most of the audience could not believe what they had just heard; but some of the audience had understood that this was the beginning of a change. I saw a gleam in the eye of *Lok* Bopharith, the district sub-governor of Snuol who had until now been unable to stop illegal army checkpoints on the road to Vietnam. Now he had heard from the Provincial Army Commander, in the presence of the First Deputy Governor, that he was authorized to put criminal soldiers in prison for six months on firearms offences – and the soldiers had heard it too.

First Deputy Governor Soem looked at me – it was up to me to round off this momentous meeting. As the colonels had been speaking, I had been wracking my brains to find a way to move the disarmament process forwards. This idea of exchanging Cambodian weapons for development projects was an innovation: no one had ever done this before, and there was no template to follow. I realised that I had to make my offer more precise, and then come back to hear their answer. Fortunately I had found a towel, which I folded under my knees to cushion the pain of kneeling, and now I raised myself again on my kneecaps.

"Conflict is a natural part of the human condition," I began. "We cannot avoid conflict between neighbours. For example, the tongue and the teeth are good neighbours who work together every day, but even so the teeth occasionally bite the tongue."

The audience laughed delightedly at the parable. I was pleased my Fulani proverb from West Africa worked well in rural Cambodia. "But we are here to avoid armed violence. If a man is angry and he takes up a stick, there will be bruises. If he has a gun, there will be death. That is why we need to apply Decree No 38 and to make sure that all illegal weapons are collected and destroyed. Remember the proverb, *a vuth man skorl chhmuos roborse via te, via skorl chhmuos te meak rong kruos punos* – an illegal firearm does not know the name of its owner; it knows only the name of its victim ... and that victim may be your own child. Therefore, if you find a weapon, you must turn it over to the police and it will be destroyed."[20]

The message was clear, but it needed to be strengthened. "I have asked you to give in your weapons, in exchange for peace.... and in exchange for development projects. Do you need a well? Or a school? Or a bridge to cross over a stream? I ask you return to your communities and discuss my offer. You will be the Ambassadors of Excellency Soem Son and of *Lok Europ*, for it is you who will be telling your communities what we are proposing. The women in particular shall be our ambassadors – for they must tell their fathers and husbands and sons that it is time for peace, time for the men to bring out the weapons and give them to the police because they are no longer needed. In peacetime, no one needs a firearm. I will return to Wat Pir Thnou in four weeks time, to hear your answer."

Now was the time for me to turn up the heat on the soldiers, and reinforce the messages of change and the Rule of Law. No one else here could challenge the army commander in public, only *Lok Europ* draped in the neutrality of the European Union.

"I believe we all realise today that we have been blessed with great honour. Not only is Excellency First Deputy Governor Soem Son presiding over the meeting, but he has brought with him some of the most important officials in the Province: the Army Commander, the Police Commander and the Gendarmerie

---

[20] I insisted repeatedly on the destruction of collected weapons, in order to to persuade civilian and military officials that this was an inevitable part of the disarmament process. In fact it took us a great deal of negotiation to convince the RGC to burn weapons, and to override military objections.

Commander. To hear such important personalities is a great honour. Now you have heard their important statements. We have all heard their statements. I am sure you have questions for *Lok* Police Colonel of and *Lok* Army Colonel. Who would like to ask a question?"

Everyone had questions, and no one would dare to ask them. So with barely a hesitation, I continued. "For example, you want to know how you can be sure that the police will protect you, if you surrender your firearms? That is a Big Question, and I will ask His Excellency the Police Commander to reply to that question."

I looked at Colonel Seng, who nodded back. "And then there is a second question to which you want an answer: how can you be sure that the local army unit will not intervene to stop the arrest of a soldier, if the police finds a soldier committing a crime? After the Colonel Seng has spoken, I will ask His Excellency the Provincial Army Commander to respond."

The army colonel avoided my eye, but Excellency Soem Son nodded approval. We needed to hear the commanders repeat their previous statements: that the police would enforce the law, and that soldiers were henceforward subject to the law. The colonels duly stood up in front of their boss the First Deputy Governor, and repeated their previous messages in answer to the questions posed by *Lok Europ.* Repetition strengthens a message. The army commander was committing his men to obey the law, and publicly giving the police permission to arrest soldiers who engaged in criminal activity. One more step had been taken on the road from civil war and armed anarchy, towards Peace and the Rule of Law.

We repeated this dog-and-pony show all week, traveling with a professional wedding catering company which provided great meals three times every day: breakfast for 30 people, lunch for 350 and dinner for 60 (for we invited local officials and police to our evening meal), each day in a different pagoda. In terms of local security, the impact of the mission was astounding. We heard no more about roadblocks, army hold-ups, or illegal hunting, and no one in Snuol District heard a gunshot during the next six months. This week Excellency Soem Son and I were traveling with an armed escort of 20 soldiers. Six months later, I traveled these same roads alone with Chou Bounine, safely perched on the back of his EU motorbike.

The return visit to Snuol District in Kracheh Province
Four weeks later I was back in Wat Pir Thnou, where the smiling monk Meah Nou with generous ears greeted me. Instead of using the courtesy title for monks *lok song,* I greeted him by name: *"chum reap sur, Meah Nou."* He laughed with pleasure. Apart from the monk himself, only I knew the monk's name (after checking my notebook). To villagers, monks are neutral prayer-leaders in orange robes, all called *lok song.* I repeatedly found that elderly monks came alive with pleasure, when I asked for their name and listened to their

personal story. My favourite was an old monk called Ho Hum, who found wisdom without ever leaving his village.

The people came in the morning, after we visitors had washed at the communal stone water jar and eaten our breakfast of rice with chicken soup. Chou Bounine arrived early, swinging in through the pagoda gate on his motorcycle with the verve of a man 40 years younger. Mr Chou was the most important person in our Weapons-for-Development programme. While I could entertain the villagers with waves of my hand and respectful *sompeat* greetings, Bounine was the real communicator. He was the person who went from village to village repeating the message, often collecting up weapons himself. Bounine was the man who liaised weekly with the local police and boosted their self-esteem. The Commune Chief arrived on his motorbike, closely followed by the six local police squeezed three to each motorbike. The police here owned three motorbikes. Since the Chief kept one for himself, it was simple arithmetic to work out how lucky it was for prestige that there wasn't a seventh policeman. They were supposed to have nine policemen in every commune, providing security for a couple of thousand people scattered through several villages. I seldom found more than six.

Finally calm was installed in the pagoda, and I greeted the one hundred and fifty assembled village representatives with my hands pressed together, *"Chum reap sur. Sob sobay teh?"* We had called for a smaller number of participants, who would report back in our second round of meetings.

I told an African proverb, and Bounine translated with animation until the villagers were laughing again and again, and clapping more and more. I distributed more coloured balloons to the infants. Now the village delegates were warmed up, they should be ready for a serious discussion of peace and disarmament. Chou Bounine used the same drawings as before, to enhance our familiar message of peace, and repeated our proverb to remind everyone about the danger of illegal weapons and explosives.

Using the pictures of children and food and health clinics we established once again, to our mutual satisfaction, that security means first and foremost food, and then health and education. The villagers were kneeling or sitting on the wooden boards of the hall, or leaning against the walls and pillars. Plastic water containers circulated. For each speaker, one of the pagoda elders had brought a coconut with a plastic straw protruding to drink the coconut milk. I sucked on my straw greedily, to sooth my throat.

"If poverty is the main source of insecurity, how can carrying weapons make you more secure?"

The idea that weapons are a source of insecurity, is counter-intuitive in a place that has known civil war for thirty years. The guy with the gun feels strong. Men feel safe, only if they are members of an armed gang that provides protection. To make peace - or to turn the 'negative peace' of a cease-fire into the 'positive peace' that brings security and an end to violence – it is essential that people accept the risk of giving up their gun. The young men in black pyjamas sitting at the back of the crowd had been born into war. Their parents and grandparents might remember peace, but the youths had known only the times when, during their childhood, they wanted a gun and the times of their adolescence when the Kalashnikov had been their companion and protector, the sign of their manhood. The whole purpose of my visit was to persuade these Cambodian villagers that they no longer needed their weapons.

At the back they crouched, men wearing dark clothes and hard, closed faces - some with the black pyjamas and red *krama* of the Khmer Rouge. Around my neck I was wearing a red *krama,* and not just because the cotton scarf went so nicely with my red shirt (although secretly I did think the color combination was rather slick). Wearing the *krama* was a deliberate choice, to show affinity with the people I was meeting. The hard-faced men would not be impressed by the red *krama,* but I wanted them to be impressed by the suggestion that giving up weapons would enhance their security and that of their families. I wanted to interest them in having wells or schools. It was essential they should convince themselves that the prestige of having schools or wells or a clinic was a better option than the risk of being arrested for keeping an illegal rifle.

Bounine-the-teacher was retelling the story of a small girl who had blown herself to pieces with her father's hand grenade, passing the microphone to women and mothers to make them express their horror to the audience. There were about 60 women sitting on the floor to the left, and as many older men on the right - my natural disarmament allies. The ones I needed to convince were the younger people sitting at the back, the men with weapons.

 "Why would people give up their weapons for nothing?" I asked them, gazing across the sea of faces. "These weapons cost money, so why should you throw them away? Perhaps you are thinking the white man with the ugly long nose and the beautiful white beard is quite mad!" The villagers laughed again. I grinned at Bounine, and moved on the next piece of the argument.

"You might say to me, 'Give me some money, and I will give you my weapon'. I say to you, 'NEVER' - for if we offer cash, all the criminals and bandits from Thailand and Burma and Vietnam will bring in weapons to sell, and we will finish up with MORE weapons in Cambodia instead of fewer weapons. If we are building peace, the last thing we want to do, is to create a new market for imported weapons!" The villagers were nodding in agreement. I watched their eyes, reassuring myself that they were not nodding off to sleep.

"So I come here today to offer you something important, in exchange for your weapons: I come to offer you peace and security. We have seen together that peace and security depend first of all on food and health. So I have come to offer you development projects, to help you produce better food for your children and better health for your mothers. In exchange you will bring us your weapons and explosives for destruction, which will create a safer and more secure environment for your families. Police protection will improve, and you will <u>help the police to protect you bet</u>ter – we will have a new security compact.[21] I came here last month to tell

---

[21] In the post-conflict environment, communities always need to develop a new sense of security. Reinforcing confidence, conveying the sense to Cambodian communities of their own empowerment, their own right and responsibility to keep the peace and to resolve differences among themselves, were essential for evolving cohesion within rural society itself. The relationship with government, police and military needed to change - the idea of 'service' inherent in 'community policing' requires as much the confidence of the people as it does the retraining of the police and military. This was our challenge.

you about the project. If you will bring the weapons, we shall destroy them and give you some development projects in exchange. I asked you to discuss with your communities, and to tell me later whether you agree. I promised that I would come back to hear your answer. I promised to come on the fourth Sunday after our last meeting. I have returned as I promised. And now I ask you to tell me if you agree to exchange weapons for development?"

Bounine handed the microphone to Suor Sdei, the Director of rural development for Kracheh province who had been chosen to lead the villagers' participation session. Bounine flopped down beside me, and drank from his coconut. I squeezed his arm and told him he had done a wonderful job. Bounine smiled happily, baring long teeth in a dark, parchment face still handsome beneath his graying hair.

In the Pir Thnou pagoda, senior village and commune leaders were stating their enthusiasm for the project. This was predictable, and meaningless. I was looking for more than words. I didn't know what I was hoping for precisely; I just knew that somewhere there must be an answer more interesting than the speech emanating from the Commune Chief's mouth: "We have heard the ideas from the Representative of Europe, and we agree with what he has said."

While Suor Sdei was looking for the next speaker, a gendarme crawled over to Bounine. Bounine leaned over to me, and started whispering: "The gendarme has informed me that five Kalashnikov AK47 rifles have been given to the head monk of the pagoda during this meeting."

I smiled at Bounine. "Well, that is a start. That makes five non-verbal 'yes' votes for a development exchange. It is not much, but it is a start."

The women were having their modest say, each agreeing that *Lok Europ's* idea was a good one - but they were women and they had no weapons to give. An old man demanded the microphone. He was dressed in black trousers with a white top, which showed he was an *achar,* an elder of his pagoda. He took the microphone from Suor Sdei and looked challengingly, first at me and then at the 150 villagers seated behind him.

"I have heard the words of *Lok Europ*, and I agree with *Europ* that it is time for peace. I have heard the promises of the Military and the Police. I know of an arms cache in the forest, up on the mountain, which contains around 300 weapons and ammunition. You can destroy these. Some of the ammunition may not be good any longer. I am willing to lead the police to the place. And I want a school for my village."

The old man sat down exhausted while I led the applause, kneeling high on my cushion. I raised my hands above my head and kept the people clapping for a full 60 seconds, and then a bit longer. Here was the response I had been waiting for, and I had better make it into a huge event.

As the applause died away and Suor Sdei took back the microphone, I leaned over to Bounine, my field officer, and said, "Now we know that the project will start. The first village to get a development project must be the village of that old man. Please find out his name and his village, and then you must arrange a visit with the local police (taking good care that the weapon cache is not booby-trapped). We shall destroy his cache in the forest, and build his village a school as soon as possible to show the other villages that weapons destroyed immediately really do bring development projects."

Bounine smiled cheerfully, and crawled across to the excited old man to collect his biographical details. I sat back in relief. The past three months of planning and travelling and speaking and negotiating and cajoling had not been in vain. The villagers living along this piece of the Ho Chi Minh trail had decided to take a risk and support the Cambodian government's peace initiative. Now all I had to do, was to persuade the Europeans to make good on their promises and fund the school.

There was no EU money in our budget for the development projects.[22] Fortunately General Henny van der Graaf had good contacts with the Netherlands Embassy in Thailand, and this produced Dutch government funding of €250 000 for WfD in Kracheh Province on the eastern frontier with Vietnam, with the NGO *Partners for Development* providing development expertise. In Pursat Province, on the western frontier with Thailand, the Japanese government offered funding, and the UNDP-RGC project known as *Seila* provided the development expertise to deliver the projects in exchange for weapons. They also supplied us with our Pursat regional Field Manager Seng Son, who became the equivalent of Mr Chou Bounine in Kracheh. Thanks to the Dutch and Japanese funding (plus useful contributions from UK and Canada for Kracheh, Germany and the World Food Programme for Pursat) the EU-ASAC programme became a success. Five years later we were able to state proudly that the Royal Government of Cambodia had destroyed 220,000 weapons by fire, of which nearly half had been collected thanks to our project.[23]

Even more critical, perhaps, our success came from 'pushing open the window of opportunity' and serving the interests of numerous different groups in different ways. In peace building, timing is often crucial. We had the support of the political hierarchy, which sought to exert control over the military – and the Prime Minister's Decree No 38 outlawing civilian weapons gave our actions critical national legitimacy. Key individuals in the Khmer political and military establishment found personal advantage in supporting us, with the EU-ASAC project bringing them prestige, office equipment, or air tickets to an international disarmament conference. We bought the support of the governors with our development projects, in provinces that were desperately poor. We bought military support by building armouries and supplying computers.[24] We won the confidence of the villagers by imposing military discipline on

---

[22] Despite having large financial resources for development projects, the European Commission staff in Phnom Penh and Bangkok were unable to adapt any projects in the National Indicative Plan (NIP) to support the EU-ASAC project, a political initiative of the Council. While it is true that Commission and Council planning cycles are different (which is a problem), their lack of support reflected attitudes of tiresome personalities and institutional jealousies at least as much as inflexible EU procedures.

[23] Counting weapons is a poor way to measure impact of the project, because the goal is actually to reduce violence and stabilize peace. This can be achieved by weapons being handed in, or buried. The only valid measurements of success are economic and commercial (see section below on evaluating WfD) and the reduction of violence.

[24] 45 weapon storage facilities were built by EU-ASAC with a total storage capability for 158,760 weapons.

the armed bands of soldiers, and we got there by bluffing our way through the public meetings with the Deputy Governor and all the colonels, and by forcing the latter to speak publicly about imposing discipline and enforcing laws.

Villagers hand over weapons to the local police, who note the details in a register book.

"You are very effective," Deputy Governor Soem Son told me over dinner, "and very humourous. But I do not know if you will succeed in burning the weapons. Soldiers like to keep firearms." Bounine translated for me, and waited expectantly. I thought carefully about my response.

"I know it is difficult for the soldiers to destroy weapons," I said. "But for the Cambodian population, it is important to see that the weapons are no longer here for war, and cannot be used by criminals for kidnapping farmers. If the Royal Government of Cambodia is able to destroy the illegal firearms, your country will have less violent crime, and the Khmer nation will become famous at the United Nations as a leader for World Peace."

Infrastructure development costs per weapon stored: €10.83 per weapon (2002 - 2005). In addition, a computerized management system was created and installed (with training for the military operators) allowing full information on weapon and munition stocks to be monitored by Military High Command and the Ministry of Defence. A Manual of Storage Procedures was created, printed and 3000 copies were distributed.

The Governor looked thoughtful. I was sure that the message would be passed along the political chain of command. Both the ruling Party and the government had interests in boosting Cambodia's international prestige. I continued: "On July 9th, 2001, the United Nations will hold a Special Session in New York, and that day has been declared International Weapon Destruction Day. It is on that date that the Royal Government should destroy the illegal collected weapons in a huge bonfire." That gave them about nine months to convince the Party and the military, and take – or impose - a difficult decision.[25]

We had the support of the international community, which wanted to stop the illegal export of weapons from Cambodia. The EU flag was also very helpful, because we could mobilize several EU ambassadors to raise any issue with the Government - and yet, despite using bilateral ambassadors to present our case, EU-ASAC continued to appear neutral because of its supra-national EU flag. '*Lok* Europ' was a neutral catalyst in every village meeting. General Henny van der Graaf, the first EU-ASAC Project Manager, and his successor David de Beer were very successful in using these levers, helped without a doubt by the fact that they both had the exalted title of Special Advisor to the European Union. This was political title for a political project, and showed the subtlety that can emerge from the political instances of the EU.

We were also subtle – and very flexible - in the way we developed new Security Sector Reform activities as the need appeared, such as building solid and purpose-designed storage facilities for military firearms which encouraged the High Command to accept weapon destruction. This flexibility (ironically) may have been one advantage of the absurd annual budget system: for while we were severely weakened by the fact that we were never certain that the project would be funded again next year, we were able to redesign the project each time we submitted the annual request for renewal.

Our strategy of persuading the Provincial Commanders to impose discipline over the military on the one hand, and bringing minimal equipment and training and self-respect to the police on the other hand, changed the balance of local security. Police posts in our pilot project areas received white boards and felt pens for their planning, and locked metal cupboards to store their office equipment and munitions (and to store more safely the volatile mortar shells and hand grenades that were handed in from time to time). To improve their community outreach, we provided bicycles, smart canvas boots and radios for their patrols, one motorcycle for their Lieutenant, and serious professional training from HQ for all police officials. Most policemen in the provinces had never received any police training. For the first time since the war, the police themselves and the citizens began to take the police seriously.

---

[25] They made it! Cambodia made a very well-received presentation to the July 2001 UN Special Session.

Local police showing new self-respect, pose with weapons they have just collected from the local community. The pyramid has been made only for the photo, and not for burning: the weapon destruction will take place later in an official public ceremony organised at the provincial level, with the Minister of Interior and Deputy Prime Minister in attendance.

At the same time we initiated income-generation activities for the police wives, to increase family incomes and make the police less dependent on bribes. The EU-ASAC final report gives the following analysis of this experiment:

> It can be estimated that the income generated for both villagers and police wives as a result of the Village Model Poultry Farms and Village Model Garden activities (implemented by the NGO Helen Keller International) has increased by between 40 - 50%. The average disposable Income in the targeted villages per household used to be approximately €1 per day, so for 15 police families and between 600 and 900 village households, the total income generated for all beneficiaries from this project since its implementation has been approximately € 615 and € 915 per month. This may seem insignificant in European terms, but represents a major injection of income for the families concerned in a country where 75% of the population are still reliant on subsistence farming for survival. ...

> The concept of providing limited economic development support to the families of police officers ... would now be considered as a counter-corruption issue, but was regarded at the time as police capacity development ... implemented with a degree of imagination, this approach could have a major role to play in future SSR and CBP development programmes in appropriate environments.[26]

In the nitty-gritty of daily field work, our WfD succeeded because we had our own staff in the field constantly talking about weapon collection, and because we involved local authorities, monks, village leaders, police and military officials in the campaign at each step. Awareness of the programme and the peace message was strengthened by our country-wide training campaign, explaining human rights and the new Cambodian weapon law, trying to reduce armed violence in the street and in the home.

This campaign was carried out by local human rights NGOs, supported by spots on the radio and by giant posters beside the road at the entrance to all major Cambodian cities. The importance of local civil society organisations (NGOs, human rights agencies, village councils, women's associations) for public awareness-raising cannot be over-emphasised. The WGWR[27] and its member organisations were crucial supporters and interpreters of the EU-ASAC message and valuable synergy was created between us. Many local NGOs had representatives in the provinces where our colleagues Chou Bounine and Seng Son worked, and they gave each other mutual support.

Every meeting Chou Bounine (in Kracheh) or Seng Son (in Pursat province) held in a rural pagoda, brought in another handful of weapons and added to the climate of confidence. The weapons delivered to the pagoda (to ensure the anonymity of donors) were handed ceremoniously to the police, who recorded their details and delivered them to the military for safekeeping. Later the RGC burned the weapons –showing that the military had ceded decision-making powers to the political authorities, and proving to the population that we were telling the truth. As the smoke rose into the sky from our Bonfires of Peace, the people of Cambodia began to believe what we were telling them: that the rule of the military assault rifle was over, that peace had finally arrived.

---

[26] Additionally, in some villages, EU-ASAC's local NGO implementing partners were able to turn the police wives into outreach agents, improving diets and enriching the whole community by teaching new poultry and horticultural techniques.

[27] *Working Group for Weapons Reduction*, a coalition of agencies supported by Oxfam and the Red Cross, which became an independent Cambodian NGO.

Weapons burning above in Kampong Thom, 25 April 2001, surrounded by sandbags for safety. On this occasion, 8475 weapons were destroyed. To generate sufficient heat to change the steel and render the weapons unusable, you need to burn a minimum of around 2,000 weapons at one time.

The first weapon destruction ceremony in April 2001 took place in Kampong Thom, Cambodia's most populous province, and this provided the breakthrough. It may have been stimulated in part by our shock declaration to the Provincial Governor, that the poor relations of his police force with the communities due to their policy of repression in Kampong Thom, made it impossible for EU-ASAC at that time to launch a pilot WfD programme in the province. The police chief was absolutely furious! But we provoked SSR progress.

While there were pressures from Cambodia's Prime Minister to gain political control over the military, other influences were also at play: such as our offer to build military armouries, our proposed support for a computerized weapon management system, and our linking of rural development projects to weapon destruction. In May 2001 certain officials were offered the chance to attend a disarmament conference in Japan, but EU-ASAC was offering to fund the air tickets and expenses only if the Cambodian delegates could tell a good story about their weapon destruction. The UN First Special Session on SALW, scheduled for July 2001, provided a strong incentive for the Ministry of Foreign Affairs to support weapon destruction – and indeed Cambodia's destruction ceremonies at Kampong Thom and elsewhere allowed the RGC to tell a very good story in New York.

Box 2: Telling the story of peace building

Our purpose has been to tell a WfD story that no one else can tell. This is a story of success, recounted as peace journalism in a form that is accessible to practitioners in the field, as well as to academics and students. Many of the readers will not be native English speakers, and we hope it is accessible to them – policemen, military personnel, customs and border officials, staff of UN and AU peace operations, NGOs and bilateral donor agencies may all be interested in how we achieved our Cambodian success.

It would be wrong to criticise the writing style too journalistic. Our peace innovation story of WfD in Cambodia is exciting, and it deserves to be read by people who want to collect weapons elsewhere. Who doesn't love a great story? We all need to understand the real story that hides behind disarmament statistics.

One day in Cambodia we received two senior and distinguished visitors to our programme coming from Europe: a EU administrator and a university disarmament professor, brilliant men. Such people influence major international decisions every year, deciding how disarmament projects are designed and financed.

Together with some Japanese colleagues from JICA, we drove for five hours through the deep puddles of the Cambodian monsoon season, to attend a village meeting with Seng Son, our Pursat Field Manager – a brave young man who was putting his life at risk every week negotiating with communities and military commanders as he collected weapons and high explosives. It was painful to watch these two Europeans struggle to understand practical disarmament. They had no idea how to talk to villagers, no concept of how villagers think and react. If we had filmed the rural pagoda that day, showing how uncomfortable these fine men felt without a suit and tie when confronted by the real work of development and peace building at the 'coal face', then readers would understand why we wish to tell our story in this way.

Ambassadors and aid officials take important decisions. Highly-educated people, they are well-briefed, intellectually brilliant and politically savvy, and yet often they create projects that fail. Decision-makers understand too little about local contexts in which they are taking decisions, and the impact of those decisions. Peace is a cultural concept: it means different things in different cultures. Although a 'cease-fire' always means 'stop shooting', its impact on women and children may not be obvious, its meaning for armed combatants may not be clear. Peace anthropology is a field that needs more research, to bring greater subtlety to project implementation.

Seen from European capitals, the sophisticated city of Phnom Penh may be seem to be 'the field' – a remote and dangerous place, probably even a hardship post. But the real action takes place 'in the field' far away from the capital city, in the tough conditions of flooded fields, poverty-bound villages and refugee camps that Western decision-makers seldom visit. Our WfD story gives something of the flavour of that work.

It is important for people like Seng Son and Chou Bounine - who travel every week across dangerous post-conflict regions on their motorbikes, who daily collect weapons from villagers, and who regularly have to negotiate eyeball-to-eyeball with armed 'terrorists' – that the people with the power and the money understand what they do. Every humanitarian frontline worker knows what we mean.

The most famous sight in Cambodia is the magnificent medieval temple complex at Angkor Wat, the largest religious complex in the world covering 162.6 acres of land. It was built in the late 11th century by the Emperor Suryavarman II and dedicated to Vishnu (but really to the Emperor himself, whose monumental carved face appears everywhere). The building of this immense vanity project probably bankrupted the country. It shows how much power and wealth were concentrated in the hands of the Khmer aristocracy and bureaucracy. Angkor Wat was converted to a Buddhist temple, which purpose it still serves, in those parts that remain in good usable condition. The tourists must be American.

4. Lessons Learned from peace building in Cambodia

Collecting weapons is pointless unless there is a favourable political context that allows disarmament to bring peace.[28] It was the politics behind our EU-ASAC programme that made WfD successful. WfD was just one part of a Security Sector Reform programme. Using a 'comprehensive, integrated security sector approach' was the heart of the success of EU-ASAC, together with the political commitment of the Royal Government of Cambodia (RGC).

Political will is all-important. RGC leaders realised they faced a major security problem, because weapons had been issued to village militias to resist the Khmer Rouge rebel remnants. Firearms were found all over the country, contributing to high levels of criminal and domestic violence. Our micro-disarmament[29] project was based on the fact that Prime Minister Hun Sen had signed Decree No 38 in 1998, making civilian weapons illegal. Weapon collection in the cities had begun before the EU became involved. The RGC did not have to be convinced of our mission. Their (and our) main challenge was to persuade local, provincial and district commanders to surrender control over their weapons – fighters who were not used to taking orders from Phnom Penh.

EU-ASAC also helped convince the government to destroy weapons. This delicate decision cemented RGC civilian control over the uniformed forces. To reinforce this key aspect of the programme, EU-ASAC established a clear connection between aid to the police and destruction of surrendered arms held in police facilities in Kracheh, Pursat and Kampong Thom provinces. To ensure destruction of surplus weapons beyond the limited pilot areas, a qualified arms and explosives expert was recruited: Colonel Adrian Sprangemeijer, former head of explosives in the Royal Dutch Army, was previously working with the Cambodian Mine Action Centre (CMAC). The 2001 EU-ASAC budget included funds sufficient for as many as ten major weapon destruction ceremonies, which allowed Col Sprangemeijer to establish direct contact with twelve of Cambodia's twenty-four governors, offering to fund a prestigious weapon burning ceremony for those governors who expressed interest. In effect we put them in competition with one another, holding out the UN's International Weapon Destruction Day on 9th July 2001 as the target date for weapon destruction: destroying weapons before that day (which they achieved) would allow the Royal Government of Cambodia, the Ministry of the Interior and the Ministry of Foreign Affairs, to present their micro-disarmament programme to the international community as a success.

At request of EU-ASAC, the Ministry of Interior and Ministry of National Defence each designated a senior officer to make up a three-person arms destruction team under the neutral EU flag. The political significance of weapon destruction was greatly enhanced by the fact the Deputy Prime Minister of Cambodia, His Excellency Sar Kheng, Minister of the Interior, presided over each destruction ceremony.

The political strategy was therefore successful. EU-ASAC provided 'financial and technical assistance'

---

[28] In 2009 the author was disarmament advisor to the United Nations in Afghanistan, at a time when the US army and NATO were importing large numbers of weapons in support of a controversial strategy to arm Afghan village militias. He therefore advised the UN to replace its weapon collection programme with weapon management.

[29] Micro-disarmament is a term used by the United Nations to cover the collection and destruction of small arms and light weapons (SALW) and their munitions and explosives. SALW are weapons light enough to be used and carried by just one or two men.

for the destruction of almost 143,000 firearms in a score of Flames of Peace[30] across the country. The bonfires of weapons convinced people that peace had truly arrived. Many of the firearms were taken from flimsy and unsecured military and police sheds and warehouses containing a mixture of weapons recently collected from civilians or from demobilised soldiers, together with surplus weapons left over from the war. Many of these weapons would have 'leaked' into the criminal market, if they had not been destroyed. Colonel Alain Perigaud, a retired French officer with previous experience in training the Cambodian military, was recruited to supervise this part of the EU-ASAC programme.

During the project period, the street price for military weapons rose 440% and there is evidence that illicit exports of hardware diminished. The micro-disarmament component of EU-ASAC must therefore have had a positive impact. Armed violence was also reduced, as shown in the Final Evaluation carried out in 2006 by disarmament expert Adrian Wilkinson:

> Data on armed violence is difficult to develop, as there are no consolidated records available from a single source. Research by the WGWR and the Small Arms Survey indicates that firearm homicide has declined dramatically from 4.0 - 5.4 per 100,000 in 1998 to 1.1 - 1.7 in 2003. This is a reduction of 70% (using mid-point levels) over a five-year period for which data is available. Qualitative evidence held in the WGWR database also suggests that this low rate of firearms homicide has been sustained over the last two years (2004 - 2005), and this is supported by hospital admission data. This shows that at the high point in 1993, 65% of victims of assault were as a result of gun shot wounds, whilst in 2004 this had fallen to as low as 2.6%. This data is supported by the analysis conducted by the Small Arms Survey of violent incidents reported in the Phnom Penh Post, which showed that the use of firearms in all violent incidents reduced from 80% (1994) to 30% (2004).
>
> By 2004, after four years of work in the field and with positive indicators that WfD had achieved its main peace objectives, EU-ASAC had transferred responsibility for weapons collection to the Communes. The Commune Council Capacity Building (CCCB) programme brought police and community leaders together for joint training – an innovative WfD exit strategy.
>
> It is not possible to state definitively that the positive impacts in reducing armed violence in Cambodia were achieved solely as the direct result of the government and EU-ASAC arms control programmes, as so many other factors, other than weapons availability and lack of controls, influence armed violence. Yet 1998 marks the beginning of the Cambodian government's efforts to remove firearms from civilian control, and 1999 saw the start of the EU-ASAC interventions. During the time in which EU-ASAC was working, there was a steady decline in armed violence in Cambodia. It is reasonable to draw the conclusion that the commitment of the Royal Government of Cambodia towards reducing the availability and proliferation of weapons, supported by EU-ASAC, has had a considerable positive impact on armed violence within the country.
> [*Adrian Wilkinson, EU-ASAC Final Evaluation 2006, Section 4.2*]

---

[30] Bonfires are not the most technically efficient way to destroy firearms, but Flames of Peace are a very effective confidence-building measure in post-conflict societies. By 2006, RGC had destroyed a total of 220,000 firearms.

Deputy Prime Minister Sar Kheng presided over each destruction ceremony, giving political weight to the weapons collection campaign and symbolically emphasising new civilian control over Cambodia's military. He and his staff wear EU-ASAC T-shirts celebrating weapon collection and destruction.

With the advantage of hindsight, we can pick out the following main lessons:

1) **Political will is critical.** If there is no political will to rid the country of illegal weapons, no voluntary weapon collection programme (VWCP) can work. In Cambodia, the Prime Minister had signed Decree No 38 in 1998, making unlicensed weapons illegal – providing a legal basis for our WfD programme and assuring the support of political authorities. One of the project's other tasks was helping the government to draft a comprehensive law on legal and illegal weapons.[31]

---

[31] Dennis Brennan was the EU-ASAC legal advisor. It is not enough to outlaw weapons: you need to draft clear regulations on firearms for legal hunters, security guards, and for the uniformed forces. Once a law is passed by parliament, regulations for its implementation have to be drafted by every ministry (rules for sailors will not the same as rules for policemen). Project design needs to allow enough time and resources to support the whole of this process which will take at least five years: otherwise the spirit of the original law may be undermined in its application by vested interests in certain ministries.

2) External catalysts are precious, but they must not interfere. There is a fine line between 'helping' and 'getting in the way'. EU-ASAC became an invaluable catalyst for the RGC, applying political pressure without ever overstepping the line. Practical peace anthropology helped our WfD work with police and military, local government officials and villagers, but we were careful never to collect any weapons ourselves: police collected them and military stored them. Weapon destruction was handled by the Cambodian political, police and military authorities, with EU technical and financial support. The weapon law was a Cambodian law, for which we provided legal expertise. EU-ASAC Programme Managers played an astute political role. In line with the Paris Principles,[32] the use of a neutral flag (EU or UN) can strengthen a national government, giving its actions legitimacy while helping it to apply international standards (for example, accountability of armed forces to the executive and legislature).

This photo shows how the weapons were stacked (all pointing in the same direction, and away from the visiting crowds) in a pyre of wood and charcoal, surrounded by a wall of sand bags 1m thick, which is enough to stop a forgotten bullet, and far enough (a generous 1 metre) from the wood-pile to allow a free flow of air to keep the fire burning for 24 hours.

---

[32] The Paris Declaration on Aid Effectiveness was endorsed on 2 March 2005 by over one hundred ministers, heads of agencies and other senior officials, committing countries and their aid organisations to increase efforts in harmonisation, alignment and managing aid for results with a set of monitorable actions and indicators.

3) **Seize the windows of opportunity: flexibility is important**. Disarmament is politics, and it is tricky. Very often you need to seize a window of opportunity, which may close if personalities or conditions change.[33] EU-ASAC used flexible EU Council procedures that proved appropriate to the needs of the mission.[34] The programme manager - with the title of Special Adviser to the EU - had an annual budget with targets to achieve. Then he was left to get on with the job. Each year he proposed new targets – thus we were able to initiate the WfD pilot projects, promote weapon destruction, fund marketing materials, contribute to the costs of Cambodian delegations attending international SALW conferences, introduce police training and support, build weapon storage facilities, etc. The EU has created flexible procedures for ECHO and the Instrument for Stability, but most EU projects are bedevilled by administrative and financial imperatives that obscure (and sometimes obstruct) the original field objectives. EU-ASAC managers had flexibility, and they proved to be very good at 'getting things done'.

4) **Development projects are not simple.** To succeed with a WfD campaign, you must have the expertise for both parts of the equation: weapons, and development. Development delivery has to be professional and participative, so that the population feels really involved in taking decisions about its own future – especially important if you want people to take decisions about whether they feel safe enough to surrender their firearms. In Cambodia, we had in PfD an excellent non-governmental organisation[35] in Kracheh Province on the Eastern Frontier, which had been dodging the bullets and running a rural development programme along the Ho Chi Minh Trail for the past five years. PfD had created village development plans in every community: the priority projects were therefore already known in each place, and the population was already organised. In Pursat Province further west, we used the Cambodian government's excellent UNDP-supported SEILA programme.[36] This shows that it doesn't matter whether the development expertise is governmental or non-governmental, although some

---

[33] For example during the 1990s, I was asked to design a VWCP for Guinea Bissau at a moment when the regime was favorable to micro-disarmament. The donor country delayed funding, and within a few months a coup d'état took place, which brought the military to power. Without donor procrastination in Europe, the disarmament project might have changed Bissau's political environment: that coup d'état (and several others) might have been avoided.

[34] EU-ASAC was established in 1999 as a Joint Action under the daily operational management of a Special Advisor serving as Programme Manager. This, says the Final Evaluation, "has many advantages in terms of the ability of a programme to respond to changing security, political and economic dynamics on the ground. This flexibility is important for SALW Control interventions because of their need to engage in the development, security and humanitarian sectors. The EU could consider this approach for future SALW Control programmes in support of national governments, where appropriate. Balanced against the above recommendation is the need for longer funding cycles." [*Adrian Wilkinson, EU-ASAC Final Evaluation Report 2006*]

[35] *Partners for Development* (PfD) – an American NGO that was originally a branch of the French NGO *Action Contre La Faim* (one of the *Freedom From Hunger* initiatives of the UN's *Food and Agriculture Organisation*), run by a very professional field director called Rick Schroeder whose well-drilling skills were learned in the oilfields of Texas. The participative community development mapping carried out by PfD was exemplary, providing an immediate implementation plan for the villagers and our WfD team.

[36] *SEILA* means 'foundation' or 'rock' and this rural development programme had a highly competent development team led by UNDP manager Scott Leiter. They had systems in place and a partnership with the rural populations with whom we were discussing disarmament and weapon destruction. Compared to PfD, SEILA was more involved in delivering development 'hardware' like roads and bridges and buildings. This did not matter for WfD, since they had a strong participative dialogue with the population to ensure that decisions were being taken together, following priorities identified by the people themselves.

Cambodian villagers felt that the development benefits arrived too slowly after they had handed over the weapons they had collected.

4. **WfD is a risky business.** The political risks of weapon collection are obvious, since it involves working in sensitive security areas and negotiating with touchy and well-armed former rebels. And the physical dangers are also very real. Cambodia had the world's highest concentration of landmines. We also quickly realised that government weapon stores were dangerous places: even police posts in the centre of towns contained piles of firearms and boxes of ammunition beside heaps of volatile grenades and mortar shells. Reorganising weapon storage was a national urgency for Cambodia, and so we adjusted project priorities and our technical capacities (recruiting a couple of colonels) accordingly.

5. **WfD requires an Amnesty.** Having made weapons illegal (the 'stick'), you need a one or two short and well-publicized periods of amnesty (the 'carrot') to encourage people to hand over weapons without fear of punishment. Some Cambodian police officers were so intent on repression and punishment, that they were unable to grasp the concept of amnesty.

6. **Police need strengthening.** People must feel secure, if you want them to hand over their weapons. In any civil war, the police force is the first institution to be destroyed: either it is wiped out, or it survives by transforming itself into a military force that abandons police work. In Cambodia in 1999, we found the police force untrained, ill equipped, and terrified of an army that acted with impunity. In our Kracheh and Pursat WfD pilot programmes we provided minimal training, equipment, uniforms and self-respect to local police, who quickly became much more effective.[37] We discovered that rural police incomes were tiny and irregular: insufficient to raise a family. To offset their need for bribes, we launched income-generation micro-projects for their wives.[38] Through political pressure, we were able to change the balance of power in the rural areas where we worked, so that police were able to intervene and impose the new firearms law, even on soldiers.

7. **Civil society is crucial for building peace.** Police cannot enforce laws without the support of the population. Using civil society organisations (CSO) to promote peace and reconciliation is an essential part of peace building, as well as using CSOs for public awareness raising and for collecting illegal weapons in every post-conflict society. Only villagers can know who may have hidden weapons. In Cambodia, our allies were the pacifist Buddhist monks, village elders working in the pagodas (both men and women), and many CSO partners with which we

---

[37] We provided radio sets, canvas boots and high quality bicycles for policemen, and one motorbike for the chief of each police post. On one occasion I remember a group of rural police trying to convince me to give them all motorbikes, which would have been too costly as well as inappropriate. "We have to carry the bicycles on our shoulders when crossing paddy fields that normally can only be crossed by bullock carts," they complained. "Very well," I replied, "I will see if I can put a bullock cart into the budget." The police looked startled and started to protest, then they saw the glint in my eye and they all burst out laughing. Humour is a vital part of negotiation.

[38] The second EU-ASAC Programme Manager, David de Beer, had a lot of development experience, and he put in place a strategy to create rather successful income-generating Village Model Poultry Farms and Village Model Garden activities for police wives, implemented by the NGO Helen Keller International. Police salaries were around $1 per day and some were as low as $15 per month, so corruption was practically inevitable simply for police to be able to feed their families.

worked. Women and women's associations play an especially important peace role, because most societies accord respect and influence to mothers and grandmothers.

8. **Government control of armed forces is vital**. In Cambodia in 1999, the biggest threat to the people was from exploitative military gangs. We tackled the issue head-on at three different levels: at the political level, at the district level, and with the Army High Command. We worked tirelessly to establish civilian political control and oversight over the armed forces – the symbol of our success was the government's decision to burn the firearms they had collected. Our offer to build proper cement-block armouries to replace their wooden storage sheds in every region (and later for every branch of the uniformed forces), provided the leverage that helped Deputy Prime Minister Sar Kheng, who was also Interior Minister, to win the power struggle with the Military High Command.[39] The government achieved better knowledge of the army's firearms and munitions stocks, and administrative control through the computer management system we established with the Ministry of Defence. From now on, the official government armouries were safe, strong and could be properly managed.

9. **Weapon destruction is a part of disarmament.** There is no better confidence-building measure for peace, than for the population to see the weapons of war being destroyed. Steel shredders are technically more efficient, but that is an expensive industrial technology that no one can witness.[40] We opted for the Flame of Peace: many thousands of Cambodians attended a score of provincial bonfires where they personally witnessed 220,000 small arms going up in smoke.[41] Storing collected weapons is not only expensive, but also inefficient because they soon start 'leaking' onto the black market. If you do not destroy the weapons you collect, you will find yourself collecting the very same firearms all over again in another conflict.[42] The definition of 'disarmament' should include 'decommissioning' and then 'destruction'.[43]

---

[39] EU-ASAC recruited a French weapons expert to run the weapon-management and storage activity: Colonel Alain Perigaud was already known to the Cambodian military as a former trainer at the Cambodian Military Academy.

[40] EU-ASAC was greatly strengthened by the fact that Prime Minister Hun Sen had initiated a disarmament campaign in 1998, with the collection of some 100,000 weapons. In 1999 a public weapon-destruction ceremony featured the PM driving a bulldozer over several thousand Kalashnikov assault rifles and crushing them. However disarmament was running out of steam in late 1999 when EU-ASAC revived the campaign.

[41] David de Beer, the second EU-ASAC programme manager, has written: "What does a Flame of Peace ceremony mean to these local people? They see thousands of weapons stacked up on a pyre waiting to be destroyed and know that each weapon played its part in the violence, death and destruction which has been part of their past and which still throws a long shadow over their present existence. And then they see the weapons engulfed by flames, in the same way as the body of a person who has just died is engulfed by flames at his or her cremation. In the Buddhist tradition, at a cremation, the failures of the past and the inadequacies of the present are laid to rest. After a Flame of Peace ceremony the weapons, recalling violence, disruption and death in this life are no more. The destruction ceremonies remain a powerful symbol, both of the Cambodian Government's intention to create a weapons free society and also reassuring the villagers that weapons they have handed in are now destroyed to increase security." [*ACPACS Conference Presentation, 1-3 April 2005*]

[42] A senior government official told the *EU-ASAC Final Evaluation* (p21): 'EU-ASAC stopped the cycle of circulation of weapons. We used to collect, they went to bad storage, they leaked and we collected them again'.

[43] Munitions and explosive stockpiles also need to be destroyed at the end of a war. This is a delicate operation requiring high military expertise and isolation. The 2006 *EU-ASAC Final Evaluation Report* emphasises that the job was not yet complete: "Of particular concern is the safety, security and control of the ammunition stockpiles within Cambodia. There are estimated to be over 100,000 tonnes of ammunition present in Cambodia, the vast

10. **A National Control Strategy is needed for SALW**. Effective management of small arms and light weapons (SALW) requires a national strategy. In Cambodia, the National SALW Commission was hampered by jealousies between Interior, Defence and the Military High Command (a frequent problem worldwide: best is to place the NatCom in the Office of the Prime Minister).[44] The UN Programme of Action (UNPoA) on SALW recommends that the Commission include all ministries concerned by SALW: health, youth and education, transport, finance (which often runs the customs service) as well as civil society organisations. A NatCom needs legal status, and a line in the national budget. Firearms are a national issue, not a military preserve. We recommend that the NatCom should have a President (probably a military officer) serving one term of five years, and an Executive Secretary changing every three years, passing from one ministry to another: so that priorities change from policing to health issues, to border controls, to education campaigns, according to the interests of each Executive Secretary. This way the NatCom remains dynamic, the issue of SALW is recognised as an issue of national concern.

11. **Codes of Conduct can be valuable for civil-military relations**. A Code of Conduct for military and police officials can transform the relationship between civilians and the uniformed forces in post-conflict societies. The Code should be based on behavioural change, supported by regulations (unlike the Cambodian case which became mired in debates about legislation). The Code needs to be supported by the Interior and Defence ministries and presented to the men and women in uniform in training sessions, rather than simply imposed by the hierarchy. Training should emphasise human rights issues, and the responsibility of officials to protect women and children. Summarising the Code's basic principles on a pocket-sized card, helps to simplify the message and ensure that key points are found in uniform jacket pockets as a constant reminder of the rules for good behaviour. [45]

12. **Advertising and education are both important.** You need a very good public awareness information campaign, to inform the population about the new weapons law, and about periods of amnesty when they can safely turn in weapons and explosives. Civil society organisations are crucial for this outreach effort, since they are both close to the people and seen as politically neutral. Radio spots as well. EU-ASAC contracted various Cambodian human rights NGOs to run training courses in towns and villages all over the country. Training sessions brought together police and military personnel as well as community leaders, teachers and Buddhist monks all working together for reconciliation and disarmament. As well as official

---

majority of which is stored in unsafe and insecure conditions." Interior Ministry officials told the evaluator that accidents from unexploded ordinance ('UXO') had gone down 50% thanks to the EU-ASAC public awareness campaign: if true, that was an unexpected positive impact. But the job had not been finished.

44 The *National Commission for the Reform and Management of Weapons and Explosives in Cambodia* (NCWMR) was formed on 21 June 2000, thanks to pressure from EU-ASAC. Led by the Ministry of Interior, the Commission does not include the Ministries of Education or Health and there is no civil society representation. The Commission meets very infrequently, is ineffective (as of 2006), and has not developed an integrated, national SALW control strategy. Its membership includes several Deputy Prime Ministers, so it is too high-level to discuss or implement useful operational issues.

45 A *Code of Conduct* (CoC) workshop was the point of departure for our message on civic responsibility, addressed both to the police and military in Cambodia. CoC training included the civilian population because all parties need to share the same principles and have the same expectations. Only if the population understands the requirements for police and military conduct, can the people even begin to try and hold these uniformed security services to account. Girls need women's organisations to support them in holding security forces accountable.

information systems, we exploited road-side billboards, printed T-shirts and tens of thousands of 'no gun' stickers to decorate cars, bikes, buses, boats and shop windows.

13. **Take your time: a campaign needs minimum five years to be effective**. Public awareness cannot be achieved nation-wide in a matter of months. We were not just marketing a slogan about 'no gun': we were trying to change social behaviour and to reduce violence in a post-war society, and aiming to strengthen civil society organisations like WGWR and human rights and lawyers associations, in order to help the government produce a new social climate in Cambodia: replace the rule of rifles with the rule of law. For such an ambitious campaign, you need to allow time for messages to reach deep into the minds of the people you are targeting. It may be comparatively easy to suppress weapons in an urban environment, given adequate political will and resources;[46] but in rural areas it is more complicated. New laws against violence take a long time to be understood and accepted, in a post-conflict society recovering from civil war. In the end, after six years of intense EU-ASAC activity, virtually all Cambodians understood that guns were now outlawed, that peace had finally arrived.

14. **EU-ASAC funded NGO education campaigns** nation-wide, training villagers and their local police and military officials about the law and about safe weapon collection and storage, and about the risks of handling explosives. Then we took the training further, talking about human rights, civil rights and domestic violence. We worked to promote radical new ideas about community policing, and changed civil-military relations by insisting on the obligations of soldiers and police officers to protect women and children in particular.

---

[46] The RGC was pretty effective in this area after the signing of Decree No 38 of June 1998. House-to-house searches were organised, road-blocks set up, key urban spaces (garages, bus stations, river ports, nightclubs, karaoke bars, and the barracks of armed forces) targeted for interception of illegal weapons.

Popular theatre was used to promote information about the dangers of weapons and their outlawed status. This is one of many ways that public awareness was improved.

15. **WfD is just one part of Security Sector Reform (SSR)**. Making peace is like a jigsaw puzzle: you cannot complete the picture if you do not have all the pieces. Collecting weapons is one piece of the jigsaw.[47] EU-ASAC was successful because it addressed a comprehensive range of Security Sector Reform (SSR) issues: writing the new arms law and drafting the rules for its implementation; training villagers, police and military about the law and its meaning; talking about human rights and the obligations of officials to protect women and children; re-training local police and supporting the concept of community policing; providing minimum police equipment;[48] working to improve legal police incomes (by helping their wives); applying discipline and legality to military possession of firearms; reforming the relations between civilians and military forces; redefining relations between soldiers and the police; improving control over weapons and ammunition; establishing civilian oversight of the armed forces; improving the storage and security of weapons and explosives at national, province and commune levels, including training in firearms security; collecting illegal weapons and offering development projects that addressed issues like rural poverty … we tackled a whole range of issues, none of which by itself would have been sufficient to make peace.[49]

16. **Criminal weapons cannot be collected through VWCP**. Armed criminal violence cannot be addressed through WfD or any other 'voluntary' scheme. The EU-ASAC mandate did not include the criminal use of weapons - therefore police forensics or weapons intelligence capability were not included. Experience beyond the Cambodian programme suggests that this is an important component of a holistic SALW control strategy, and more strengthening of police capacities could be important in future interventions for weapon management and control.

17. **WfD success should be measured by renewed economic activity.** WfD is a peacebuilding programme. The objective is 'peace'. The actual number of weapons collected is not too important (even with the best surveys and baseline studies, we have no idea of how many illegal weapons and explosives are out there in weapon caches). Weapon collection is intended to stop weapon misuse – it matters less whether a rifle may surrendered to a policeman or buried in a rice field, than that the weapon is no longer being used. If WfD is successful, increased traffic flows will indicate that the roads are safe; busy markets will prove that people are trading; new building investment will show that people now believe in peace; reduced criminal action or domestic violence involving firearms (and increased blackmarket prices for firearms) will indicate that weapons are going out of use. Those are the best ways to judge the success of WfD.

---

[47] Another piece of the SSR jigsaw is Disarmament and Demobilisation of former rebel fighters, and their Reintegration into society (known as DDR, or *RDRDRDR* = 3D4R). This activity was being carried out by the RGC with support from the UN's World Bank and World Food Programme. EU-ASAC was not involved.

[48] Motor bikes, VTT/ATB pedal bikes, two-way radios, decent boots, lockable steel cupboards, white boards for activity planning all improved their self-respect, effectiveness and visibility, and we funded basic police training.

[49] The Recommendations in the 2006 EU-ASAC Final Evaluation Report include the following: "Future SALW Control programmes of the EU should not constrain themselves to just specific functional areas of SALW Control such as weapons collection or weapons destruction. They should be provided with the mandate and capability to engage in all areas of SALW Control, as holistic and integrated strategies and responses are more efficient, effective and have longer-term impact."

18. **Evaluating a VCWP should include a wide range of opinions.** Since 'peace' is the objective, the opinions of the general public and the security forces should be given more weight than those of ministers and ambassadors, when it comes to judging the success of a weapon collection programme. The judgement of high officials may be influenced more by financial or political factors, than by the reality of peace building in the field.[50]

19. **Disarmament costs time and money, but it is much cheaper than war.** You cannot 'do' WfD in a few months. A disarmament project takes years to mature and obtain an impact.[51] The project cycle for WfD and Security Sector Reform is more than 6-7 years. One of the oddities of the EU-ASAC project was its funding by the EU Council on an annual basis, initially without money for activities.[52] The European Commission had adequate resources to fund WfD, but EC officials in Phnom Penh and Bangkok refused support because EU-ASAC was created by the EU Council of Ministers.[53] The Japanese government provided funds for the Pursat pilot programme, but EC development officials in the region did not understand the importance of EU-ASAC. After we implemented the two WfD pilot projects in Kracheh and Pursat provinces (costing between €250,000 and €300,000 each, which is really extremely modest in terms of peace budgets[54]), EU-ASAC experimented with using local NGOs to build cheaper wells. In terms of weapon-collection 'WfD-lite' was less spectacular than the larger projects; but 'success' must be measured using economic indicators. Probably 'wells-for-weapons' was only possible because the two larger pilot projects had already helped to change the mood in the country. It is clear with hindsight, that we persuaded the RGC to destroy collected and surplus weapons only by offering substantial development assistance to tackle poverty in Kracheh and Pursat, and by building solid, prestigious weapon storage facilities for the provincial army commanders.

---

[50] Mozambique provided a good example of UN Security Council ambassadors closing a weapon collection programme too early, without providing time and money for weapon destruction. The UN experts were pulled out, leaving registered weapons in storage: providing data to prove that many armed criminals throughout Southern Africa subsequently obtained weapons that the UN had collected in Mozambique. See Note 3.

[51] For example, the DDR component of the *Afghan New Beginnings Programme* was designed to disarm 100,000 combatants in only three years. In reality, however, it required 18 months to build the team (experienced military and civilian personnel) and purchase the equipment (trucks etc for safe transport, storage and destroying up to 100,000 firearms and unknown quantities of ammunition): which left just 18 months for the real DDR activity. The result of 3-year funding was a 'military' planning structure, neglect of the 'R' components, and no provision for long-term follow-up action, monitoring or evaluation. Donors misunderstood the WfD/SSR 6-7 year project cycle.

[52] "The adoption of an annual funding mechanism constrained the ability of the EU-ASAC programme to deliver long-term WfD strategies, or to engage in any longer term activities to control weapons within Cambodia. It is now generally accepted that impact of SALW Control programmes are mid- to long-term in nature and therefore should be supported by multi-year funding mechanisms. (Indeed the very success of EU-ASAC shows the impact that sustainable funding can have - but it can be more efficiently and effectively committed if allocated on a multi-year basis)." [*Adrian Wilkinson, EU-ASAC Final Evaluation Report 2006*]

[53] Institutional programming differences are partly responsible for this situation: the EC *Country Strategy* and *National Indicative Programme* (NIP) contained no provision for SALW activities. This does not explain why we were refused use of the EC Delegation conference room for meetings with government officials (we had to hire hotel conference rooms instead). The launch in 2011 of the new EU External Action Service should improve the overall harmony of EU activities in the medium term.

[54] The EU-ASAC core budget of €1 mil per year was also tiny compared to other peace operations, and gave very good value for money.

20. **The project cycle can be misleading.** An unexpected criticism in the EU-ASAC *Final Evaluation Report* was that the success of the project has misled the international community into believing that the SALW problem in Cambodia was fixed and finished after six years. In fact there is considerable suspicion that after the closure of EU-ASAC, local army commanders were happy to see the computer management system for weapons break down (as happened two years later); that improvements in police corruption may wither away; that five years is too short a period to install community policing and durable human rights values; that the destruction of surplus firearms and munition stockpiles may cease; that the National Commission may never be functional without continued international pressure; that civil society influence and expertise may wane … Indeed the famous Cambodian *Working Group for Weapons Reduction* (WGWR) – an existing network of 70 NGOs engaged in SALW and Armed Violence Prevention which gained in strength, expertise and influence thanks to support from EU-ASAC – appears to have faded and folded. 'Declaring victory' and 'closing a project' may therefore be self-defeating. EU-ASAC was launched not only because SALW was an issue for Cambodia, but also because Cambodian SALW management posed serious concerns for stability throughout South-East Asia. Long-term foreign policy objectives should take precedence over the short-term project cycle. 'Exit Strategies' may be short-sighted.

21. **Using film provides a great communication and reporting system.** Pictures are stronger than words. While written six-monthly narrative reports and monthly financial reports are necessary, they will never have the same impact as a 30-minute film. One of the lessons of EU-ASAC is that every peacebuilding programme should produce video documentation, and include that cost in the initial budget. Impact evaluations are best presented on film. EU-ASAC created short videos to show villagers the benefits of WfD. The Dutch government also funded a documentary film about EU-ASAC and WfD, that was shown at the first UN Conference on small arms in July 2001, and had a huge impact.
This film created by director Sander Francken can be enjoyed at:
http://www.cultureunplugged.com/play/4369/Fighting-Weapons-for-Development

Box 3: Spending EU money more efficiently

Despite its success, the EU-ASAC project was only funded on an annual basis – meaning that we could never be certain we would be able to continue work next year. We were never sure that we would be able to keep our promises to the Cambodian government or to the communities. We had to defend our existence in Brussels every nine months, simply to survive for another year. While EU funds were voted to pay the core team, little funding was provided for planned activities. Given this handicap, it is surprising that the project kept going for six years and achieved so much.

The need to reapply for funds every year forced the Project Manager to spend around 30% of his time on fundraising. For the WfD pilot projects, the EU supplied no money at all. We ourselves found the Dutch and Japanese money for WfD, but we did not know in advance where we would find money. I made my WfD commitments to the Governors and villagers of Kracheh and Pursat provinces without knowing if I could deliver on my promises. The Dutch money came thanks to General Henny van der Graaf's good relations with his Embassy in Bangkok. The Japanese money was obtained through the good offices of the Japanese Ambassador in Geneva whom I knew through UNIDIR, and who was willing to phone Tokyo to support a funding request from the Japanese Embassy in Phnom Penh.

Because the budget was inadequate, we spent much of our time writing funding applications and convincing ambassadors about the value of our work: indeed the Japanese Embassy funded us because they were impressed by our WfD strategy, and in order to stop the flood of illegal weapon exports from Cambodia; and later they created their own project modelled on ours. Perhaps the permanent fight for funding was an advantage; but I think not. As well as wasting management time, the project manager and the EU repeatedly 'lost face' with Cambodian officials because our very existence was so uncertain from one year to the next, giving us very little funding flexibility.

If Western officials had an efficient understanding of the grassroots processes for building peace, disarmament and reconciliation, they would respect the project cycle and would never fund a programme for just twelve months. The standard so-called EC 'project cycle' is really a 3-year accounting cycle, which has nothing to do with the reality of project cycles in the field.

EU officials should approve budgets for at least seven years (15-year 'programmes' would make more sense than 3-year 'projects'): requiring monthly accounts to show **efficiency**; six-monthly 'effectiveness reports' to explain effective **results**; and every three years they should monitor the **impact** of expenditures. This long-term approach would allow the project team to focus their efforts on obtaining good results and positive impacts.

5. Weapon Management Checklist

Not every country can outlaw civilian weapons. Peace is cultural. While Cambodia decided to ban civilian weapons, many Texans and Afghans, Yemenis and Albanians consider carrying firearms to be a sign of manhood: there is little point in building a 'disarmament' strategy in such cultures where 'managing firearms' may be more appropriate. This could include licensing weapons, while making it a crime to possess grenades, or military explosives; private ownership of military assault rifles may also be outlawed, since no sportsman can claim that the AK47 is an ideal weapon for shooting rabbits.

Some version of WfD[55] could usefully be part of a weapon management strategy. We offer the following Weapon Management Check-list as a helpful memorandum and guide for practitioners.

All collected and surplus weapons need to be destroyed, to avoid their falling to the wrong hands. This looks like a piece of metal junk, but it is in fact a sawn-off AK-47 military assault rifle, deliberately transformed into an easily concealable one-shot lethal weapon for criminal use in Cambodia.

---

[55] EPES Mandala is one of the very few groups with practical experience of using field-tested and successful methodologies for collecting and destroying SALW. Since General Henny and Dr Poulton are founders of the EPES Mandala, it is no exaggeration to say that we created the concept of WfD and made it work. WfD and its offshoots have been used in a number of countries and with numerous cultural permutations. It has now entered the common vocabulary of disarmament and become a part of the general knowledge of peace building.

What Weapon Management should include:

- legislation to clarify who is allowed to carry or own what type of weapon, and for what purpose (together with regulations for the implementation of the legislation by each ministry);
- strict laws to control the buying and selling and possession (safe storage) of firearms and ammunition, and all forms of explosive material;
- clear definitions of 'firearms' so that the rules are evident to all;
- clear distinctions between 'hunting' and 'military' weapons, and hand guns;
- special rules governing handguns, which are not 'hunting weapons'.
- repression of military weapons, so that private citizens and licensed security guards may own and carry only 'reasonable' arms;
- strict controls over the use, storage, carrying and transport of all legal military and police and security weapons and ammunition;
- strict rules about all weapon storage, and the separate storage of munitions;
- strict rules about who may buy or sell or import ammunition;
- strict rules to control access to military and civilian (mining) explosives;
- ensuring that military and police weapons are carried only by people on duty and in uniform;
- transfer of civilian weapon policing responsibility from soldiers to police forces;
- training police and customs officials to ensure they know and understand the rules and legislation on firearms, and how they should enforce them;
- support to the police, to ensure that they have the mandate, political support, expertise and minimum resources necessary to carry out their tasks;
- support of police weapon-management actions by judiciary, politicians and military, with removal of all 'impunity' for corruption or misuse of weapons;
- registration of firearms, so any 'illegal' weapons can be made 'legal' or removed,
- major public awareness campaigns on the law and on the dangers of firearms;
- public awareness campaigns about the dangers of handling explosives;
- mobilisation of women's and lawyers' associations, civil society, religious and other opinion leaders to promote awareness about weapons and the law;
- repression of illegal firearms through policing (check points, searches, etc);
- strong border controls, with expertise training and awareness of customs officers to repress weapon and ammunition smuggling;
- joint training of border guards, police and other weapon management officials, to promote excellence and inter-agency cooperation;
- promoting cross-border collaboration and the harmonising of weapon legislation between neighbouring States, and the common application of rules and laws;
- voluntary collection by police of illegal weapons and munitions (including periodic amnesties to encourage people to hand over 'newly discovered' firearms and explosives without fear of arrest);

- registration and destruction by police of illegal weapons (to avoid illegal resale or 'leakage');
- destruction by government of surplus and outdated stocks of weapons and ammunition (to avoid resale or 'leakage' – for firearms surplus to military use or that work poorly, can still be recycled as dangerous criminal weapons);
- destruction by trained military experts of collected ammunition and explosives (to avoid 'leakage' and accidental explosions);
- careful, accountable management of government armouries and stockpiles;
- regular and rigorous external audits of government armouries;
- strict licensing and control of all imports or exports of firearms, explosives and ammunition;
- licensing and control of all arms manufacture, including artisans;
- licensing and control and regular inspections of all guard and security companies;
- individual licensing and training for all guards approved for carrying weapons;
- background checks / morality certification for all applications for gun licences;
- licences should be allocated only with signed approval of a local village Elder and the local police chief;
- licences and morality checks should include signed approval by spouses (notably in case of men with a record of violence): spouses should have power of veto;
- seizing of weapons and refusal of licenses to men who are guilty of domestic or social violence;
- seizing of weapons and refusal of licenses to men who are guilty of crimes;
- this checklist implies a recognition that elimination of firearms is unrealistic in certain societies; and if guns cannot be removed from society, then **weapon management can be an acceptable alternative,** with weapons either licensed, surrendered, buried or hidden (any of which represents progress compared to a post-conflict environment where firearms are used daily to cause fear and to extort payments from people).

Conditions for Weapon Management success:

-   weapon management accepts that society contains weapons, and that they should be subject to reasonable control;
-   weapon management requires a political consensus seeking to ensure social harmony and individual safety;
-   weapon management must be accepted by the population as a reasonable policy, a trade-off between the freedom (mostly of men) to shoot and the freedom (often of women and children) not to be shot;
-   weapon management therefore needs the involvement of civil society organisations (CSO) which develop expertise in this field in order to work with the population, and with the relevant government ministries and departments;
-   weapon management requires concerted government action of all concerned ministries (which includes health, education, transport, finance, etc) as well as the uniformed forces;
-   the UN Programme of Action on small arms (UNPoA) insists on the importance of a National Firearms Commission acting as a focal point for national and international cooperation on small arms management; we recommend that this Commission of technicians be placed in the Prime Minister's office, and be the 'round-table' at which national weapon policies can be discussed and elaborated between technical experts, who will then formulate proposals for the political decision-makers.
-   weapon management requires rigorous and honest police forces and border controls enforcing clear and accepted laws and rules;
-   weapon management requires that police actions should be supported by government, politicians and judiciary, showing concerted political will by central government and local authorities throughout the land;
-   weapon management can only work if registration and enforcement are applied at the lowest administrative (district or commune) level;
-   weapon management licensing requires grassroots participation, for only local people know which of their neighbours can be trusted with a weapon;
-   weapon management therefore requires widespread information about the laws;
-   weapon management can be strengthened by regional and national databases, but only if the decentralized registration system is efficient and provides good data. Experience shows it is very easy to fail with a centralized system; or to create an expensive computerized database filled with useless names, containing out-of-date information that no one can use or even access.

In the past, development agencies have shied away from anything approaching weapons and security – and yet experiences since the 1990s (especially in Africa) have established that 'security is a development cost'. The EU has been more flexible that many other donor organisations, in recognising that economic and social development is impossible without the assurance of a minimum level of security.

The argument runs that if you want to promote economic development, you need 'security first'… or at least a minimum and adequate level of security. Security is therefore a development cost.

Weapon-exchange strategies like WfD and WED, offer micro-projects to rural communities, overtly in exchange for firearms and in order to obtain greater security. This recognises the link between poverty and violence that was extremely evident in the Kracheh pilot project described in detail above. While poverty may often be a cause of social unrest, poverty is always and inevitably a consequence of civil war. We are dealing with both guns and people. Any agency dealing with micro-disarmament in rural post-conflict communities, needs to help build security by strengthening local police and by rebuilding the micro-economy at the very same time.

Some development experts are uneasy with disarmament. The 'weapons linked to development' (WLD) proponents argue that separate micro-disarmament projects are inefficient. VWCP should be integrated into existing development activities. SALW becomes one of many development incentives.

Against this argument must be set the reality that firearms and explosives involve risks of a different nature to credit programmes, schools, health or irrigation. All may be related to good governance and development, but they are not all the same. Micro-disarmament is not like micro-credit. Only trained military professionals can deal with the technical aspects and physical danger of firearms and explosives. Soldiers only trust other soldiers.

There is also a political issue, for police and military authorities always want to control weapon-related activities. This can be a problem, since weapons also involve obvious health, education, transportation and other questions. The issue of weapons in society is not exclusively a military affair. For this reason, the UN Programme of Action on small arms and light weapons (UNPoA) recommends the creation of a National Commission or National Focal Point, where all ministries – together with civil society – meet to establish common policies towards SALW and explosives. All countries have signed up to the UNPoA, so governments and donor agencies ought to be open and flexible to WfD. Development experts are seldom involved with the National Commission: which strengthens the argument for having specific micro-disarmament programmes that focus on 'security first'.

The reality is that every sector requires high levels of expertise. WfD has the advantage that it brings military experts into partnership with social scientists. We need engineers for roads, drillers for wells, seed specialists for agriculture… and bomb-disposal experts to destroy ammunition caches. In the past, SALW have been the entry point for security sector reform with the police and the military; but they can also be an entry point (in certain post-conflict societies) for economic development, as the Cambodian story illustrates.

The EU-ASAC experience we have described, shows that micro-disarmament is effective as a peace building activity only when it is a part of a comprehensive programme that includes other SSR and economic development investments. Building peace is like putting together a jigsaw puzzle: one or two pieces alone cannot provide the whole picture…. And when one or two pieces are missing, the picture cannot be completed.

Programmes need to be designed with this holistic approach in mind. WfD, WED, WLD or whichever variant you favour, will not produce good results unless the other pieces of the jigsaw are in place. Building peace requires political will to provide good inter-ministerial cooperation, together with good inter-agency collaboration and good involvement of civil society – sometimes the three pieces of the jigsaw most needed to complete the picture.

Sunset over the Royal Palace and the Tonle Sap River in Phnom Penh, capital of Cambodia – a beautiful country.

6. Evaluating Weapon Programmes

The Goals of weapon management and WfD are to promote conditions for lasting peace and economic revival, by removing or reducing armed violence in a post-conflict society.

The key measurements of WfD and VWCP success are economic: removing violence allows societies to prosper, recreating a trade and investment economy where firearms have no place. A weapon collection programme should be judged not by the numbers of weapons and ammunition collected and destroyed, but by whether firearm-related violence is reduced and economic development has restarted. Collecting and destroying illegal weapons is 'good' but not sufficient: it is the economic peace benefit that justifies the costs of disarmament. With total weapon numbers unknowable, counting collected weapons is a poor indicator of success.

The Measurable Results of WfD are therefore: a reduction in the use of firearms and explosives, leading to:

- greater popular confidence in the reality and durability of peace
- fewer incidents of social and domestic armed violence
- fewer incidents of violent crime
- more traffic on the roads
- more trade with bigger and active markets
- more economic investment

The Measurable Outcomes and **Impact** of WfD are best be assessed through proxy indicators that can be monitored over a period of three to seven years, using a variety of measuring systems.

-**Outcome:** Illegal use of firearms declines (police and press reports, opinion surveys)
-**Outcome:** police forces function better locally, while at the same time civil-uniformed relations improve[56] (police and press reports and local opinion surveys);
-**Outcome:** weapons are collected, recorded and stored (police records, audits of weapon storage);
-**Outcome:** firearms availability declines (crime records, price surveys for weapons/munitions);
-**Outcome:** collected weapons are destroyed, reinforcing peace and avoiding 'leakage' (press reports; photos; official reports and audits of weapons collected, stored and destroyed);[57]
-**Outcome:** a greater sense of security obtains in the country (opinion survey, crime statistics);
-**Outcome:** confidence in peace increases among the population (opinion survey, spending patterns);
-**Outcome:** freer circulation of goods and people, roads and markets are more frequented (traffic surveys, market tax accounts and market attendance records);[58]

---

[56] Better police performance may be an outcome of WfD/SSR, but it is also necessary for WfD success

[57] Provided that WfD is part of a broader SSR programme, there may be strong parliamentary oversight of the armed forces, audits and good management of military stores and armouries, etc. that are not direct outcomes of WfD. Nor will be possible to affirm that better circulation of people and trade are solely due to WfD; but the 'security first' doctrine suggests that such positive economic outcomes will not occur without weapon collection.

[58] For example in Cambodia, one positive result of WfD in terms of community social and economic development was cutting the journey time from Phnom Penh to Snuol from 1.5 days to approximately 4 hours. This had

-**Outcome:** increased trade and prosperity, people begin to invest locally (press and local government reports, transport, building and economic surveys, household spending patterns);
-**Outcome:** greater social and economic development takes place, school and clinics re-open and function (ministry reports, press reports, economic and social surveys);
-**Outcome:** improved local governance, as leaders, police and justices apply laws, collect and destroy illegal weapons while accepting responsibility for the registration and careful management of those weapons that are allowed under the law, including their own well-controlled armouries (reports, surveys, press analysis, weapon registration logs, audits of weapon storage).[59]

Incidents of crime and armed violence can be measured using police statistics: data-recording will be an important part of the police capacity strengthening that needs to accompany WfD actions. Transport and other economic information can be used to appreciate the economic impact of peace and WfD. These proxy indicators - monitored over a period of three to seven years - are definitely better WfD indicators than simply counting weapons. On the other hand recording firearms and ammunition is the only way to verify weapon management and destruction, which we consider a necessary and integral part of the disarmament process. Popular belief and confidence in peace can be measured by 'before and after' surveys – and if there was no pre-project baseline conducted, then opinion surveys should ask people how they feel now and to compare this with how they remember feeling earlier. It is essential to carry out surveys of women's opinions, and separately from the men.

There are standard formulae for donor-funded evaluations, carried out by external experts. Do these evaluation criteria take account of popular perceptions, or do they focus only on government officials? UNDIR has tested Participatory Monitoring and Evaluation (PM&E) methodology[60] to evaluate the impact of weapon collection and Weapons for Development programmes, asking the beneficiaries in the field (women especially, but also village men, police and leaders) their opinion of WfD impact. Women judge WfD impacts very differently from colonels.

What we are proposing is a distinction between 'results' or activities, and 'impact'. It is too easy to count wells or weapons, without wondering whether the project has achieved the desired health and peace impacts.

It is important that the administrative monitoring of activities and expenditures (how many weapons, how many villages, how many development projects, how much money, how many signed receipts) should not dominate the evaluation of impact; and the latter should take notice of what local people think and feel. Eleanor O'Gorman emphasises that UN and other interactions with local people need to be dynamic, treating the local population as actors rather than as passive recipients or 'targets' of assistance – and we should recognize that impacts may be positive or negative. She observes that, "a local human rights activist being funded by a Western aid agency may

---

beneficial impacts on social and living conditions, and probably on security as well since access for police was similarly improved. We saw businessmen building new shops and hotels. The road development was supported by the WFP, working in partnership with EU-ASAC: 121 tonnes of rice were provided to build 6.85 kilometres of road in Pursat, and 100 tonnes of rice for 5 sections of road in Kracheh.

[59] An explosion or a fire in an arms depot means one of two things: either the depot was poorly managed and officers were negligent; or there has been large-scale theft of weapons, explosives and ammunition, and the purpose of the fire was to destroy evidence of corruption.

[60] See Robert Muggah: *Listening for Change! Participatory Evaluations of DDR and Arms Reduction in Mali, Cambodia and Albania*. Small Arms Survey, University of Geneva and UNDIR: April 2005; see also Geofrey Mugumya and Shukoko Koyama: *Exchanging Weapons for Development in Cambodia – an assessment of weapon collection strategies by local people*. UNIDIR Geneva: March 2005.

also be a village elder, locally elected councillor, and relative of the local warlord."[61] Such a fluid analysis is particularly relevant in WfD programmes: their impact should be measured not only using academic statistical measurements that seem evident to the Western evaluator, but also through the eyes and experiences of men and women (especially women) and youths in the villages and urban slums, using the values that are important to them. These are the people – after all –for whom peace building is being undertaken.

---

[61] O'Gorman, Eleanor: *Conflict and Development – development matters.* ZED Books: London 2011, p118. On the question of the domination by Western experts of the peace and development discourse, see also Pouligny, Béatrice: *Peace Operations Seen From Below.* Hurst & Co: London 2006; and Kothari, Uma, 'Authority and expertise: the professionalisation of international development and the ordering of dissent', in *Antipodes* 37 (3), p425-46, both cited by O'Gorman in her discussion of local engagement and ownership of peace processes.

Conclusion

Reducing the use of firearms is essential for building peace after any prolonged civil conflict. Some form of voluntary weapon collection programme usually has a significant role to play, so exchanging weapons for development (or other incentives) is one useful option to consider. It is also important to recognise the limitations of micro-disarmament, which is just one action towards building peace. While the nature of VWCP and WfD is political, their most important impact is economic. **EPES Mandala Consulting** is convinced by long field experience that micro-disarmament and weapon destruction should be a part of every programme that seeks to transform a state of war into a culture of 'positive peace' – but WfD is only one piece of Security Sector Reform.

Peace is a cultural concept. In Cambodia in the late 1990s, gang rule replaced civil war and the State needed to gain control over provincial colonels who were *de facto* warlords. Our story shows how the EU-ASAC project played a role both in reducing armed violence in post-conflict Cambodia, and in helping the civilian government to gain political control of the Cambodian armed forces by 2006 (the public burning of surplus and outdated military weapons was one of the ways in which this political control was asserted).

WfD civilian disarmament was a successful part of the Cambodian government's gun-free policy, and that is the story we have told. But voluntary weapon collection will not work everywhere: in a land like Afghanistan, where 'women wear jewelry and men wear guns', outlawing weapons is not realistic. In such cases, weapon collection should be replaced by a strategy of weapon management. In all cases, rebuilding the police and re-establishing confidence in local governance systems is vital. WfD will contribute to durable peace, only if it is a part of a comprehensive security sector approach with strong political leadership, and a commitment to decentralised economic development. The same conditions influence out-migration, which is caused by conditions of physical insecurity, and by the poverty and economic insecurity that conflict produces.

Responsibility for peace and disarmament must be shared with civil society organisations and local community institutions. Local police units will only help peace to flourish if they are efficient and honest, and if they work as allies of the local governance leaders, including mayors and CSOs. Permanent peace will flourish only in a society where State institutions function in a transparent manner at the decentralised level, and show themselves capable of assuring an acceptable level of security and prosperity for their people.

The origins of EPES Mandala Consulting

The Founders debated for several years before deciding to create a consulting company in 2004. From Timbuktu to Freetown, from Yugoslavia to Afghanistan, from Sri Lanka back to Rwanda and Liberia, we were involved in some of the most vicious trouble spots (not forgetting Darfur). Since then we have worked in many other countries as assessors, monitors, evaluators, trainers and sometimes as implementers of peace-related and disaster-relief programmes, adding to our experience by learning in places like Cambodia, Indonesia, Haiti, Somalia, Sudan, Central Africa, DRC and Middle East. From our collective experience, we believe we have worked out some solutions.

We specialize in the complex niches of governance and security sector reform (SSR), weapon management and control, conflict early warning and early intervention leading to sustainable peace building. We add development to disarmament, offering non-military solutions for collecting and destroying weapons as part of an overall plan of action to build peace. The programmes are always complex, often dangerous, but you must take risks to create peace.

Peace is good for business. Sustainable development creates the conditions for sustained peace, just as poverty and exclusion create the conditions that promote violence and terrorism, outmigration and refugees, weak institutions and failed states.

Box 5. Mandala, symbol of harmony and sustainable peace

The Mandala is a prayer circle, symbolizing harmony in the Buddhist tradition. The use of this word in our company's name, represents our distrust of Western linear thinking in the field of peace building.

Circular modes of reasoning help us harmonise our analyses with the thinking of the peoples in whose countries we are privileged to be working. The Mandala also inspires our company logo, which shows the original Flame of Peace – 27 March 1996 in Timbuktu, Mali - contained inside a mandala circle of peace and harmony.

EPES Mandala recognises that peace brings economic development, and vice versa. Our conflict transformation strategies assume that post-conflict disarmament actions will give way to economic development activities. There is no smooth progression, but it has to happen. Yesterday's small arms emergency will become tomorrow's development opportunity. Through our wide experience, the EPES Mandala team has evolved strategies for conflict transformation that takes the disarmament project forward from security to development.

o We address the structures of the social economy using participative action-research methodologies.

o We attack all aspects of SSR and DDR (3D4R) together, transforming conflict into peace.

o We rebuild government administrative and security institutions, while working with civil society organisations and decentralized governance to bring citizens into the economic and political process.

o Our recruitment and management insist on the need for rigour, and our staffs are constantly challenging their original assumptions. Societies are not static, and neither are we.

****

EPES Mandala Consulting Ltd

U.S. Office: Dr R.E. Poulton
1636 West Grace St, Richmond
Virginia 23220, U.S.A.
repoulton@epesmandala.com
poultonrobin@gmail.com

Brussels Office: Mr Olivier Pêtre
500 Avenue Louise
1050 Brussels, Belgium
office@epesmandala.com